The Power of Forgiveness

Release the Elephant off Your Back

R. T. Kagels

Table of Contents

Introduction

Resentment is like drinking poison and hoping your enemy dies. –Nelson Mandela

There are a few versions of the above quote, but the point that they get across is the same. The quote is accredited to several people, but there doesn't seem to be agreement on the origin. However, it is not who said it first that is important, but rather what was said. It reads as follows (McKenna, n.d.):

There are several variations of the quote as well. However, the message is the same: resentment is only going to hurt you. This is the case with anger, hate, or any other negative emotion directed at another person. So, why do so many of us harbor animosity and refuse to let it go? There is no simple answer to that question, and some may argue that we don't have to answer it. Either way, forgiveness is the tool that can lift the weight of negativity that we place on ourselves by refusing to forgive, whether consciously or subconsciously.

Practicing forgiveness is not easy, even when it comes to forgiving ourselves, but there are a number of steps that can be put in place to facilitate the process. Letting go of grudges and releasing toxic feelings toward others leads to personal healing, inner serenity, and stronger interpersonal relationships. Gaining the skills needed to forgive will have a profoundly positive impact on your emotional well-being and quality of life.

I can speak from experience when I say that letting go of emotional burdens through forgiveness turned my life around, and some life it has been...so far. I have worked as a musician, a shipyard electrician, and an industrial millwright. I have owned a limousine company, and I have owned a real estate investment company". As well as being a licensed commercial instrument pilot. My past has taught me many things, and I would be mistaken if I told you that I have never had enemies, never treated people badly, never held on to anger, and never done anything that I am not proud of. It is a very rare breed of person that can honestly say they haven't fallen victim to any negativity. On the other side of the coin, I have been the subject of other people's anger and have been treated badly myself, but I have also received kindness and love, just like I have given kindness and love.

Due to my array of experiences across so many areas of life and the wisdom that they have left me with, in addition to being told on numerous occasions that I should write a book, I have decided to do just that. My goal is to give you a helping hand by calling on the things that I have been through and the measures that I managed to put in place to harness the power of forgiveness, release that elephant from my back, and live a life of enrichment, fulfillment, and peace.

In the chapters that follow, you will learn to understand forgiveness and the psychology behind the inability to let go of grudges. There are several myths about forgiving, which will be debunked, including the differentiation between forgiveness and reconciliation. You may find it interesting that holding onto emotional hurt can manifest physically, and we will explore that concept, in addition to looking at brain patterns, mental health, and boundaries, followed by a real-life story of a relationship that was torn apart due to a lack of forgiveness.

Stress is a phenomenon that we all experience, and there is a palpable link between stress and the inability to forgive. The knock-on effects can be poor sleep, a compromised immune system, and chronic pain, among others. The aforementioned are all topics of focus, as are depression, negative rumination, and clouded decision-making under the weight of emotional strain.

The good news is that healing is possible by recognizing needs, embracing vulnerability, and seeking support. You can look forward to acquiring these skills and becoming brave enough to confront rocky emotional terrain. Friends and family have been there to support me, and I will explain how you, too, can educate your loved ones on the kind of support that you require. We will discuss outside help from therapists and support groups, as well as literature and educational media content that aids and emphasizes the process of forgiveness.

As you know, letting go is vital, and we will hone in on this concept by breaking it down. You can anticipate explanations of introspective thinking and action, including journaling, mindfulness, meditation, and other positive outlets. These methods are all geared toward living in the present through mental aptitude, part of which is finding calm in mental chaos. Don't underestimate art and music to soothe resentment and promote its release, along with telling your stories and hearing the stories of others, which concepts you will become familiar with.

Then, we turn to look at setbacks, the power of cognition, and explanations of *why* memories resurface in what appears to be a subconscious effort to maintain ties to the past. With an understanding thereof, you will gain further knowledge about reframing negative thoughts, self-reflection, and regular checks and balances to monitor progress along the road to forgiveness.

It is common that our past informs our future, and how we view the past through feelings and emotions is what guides either a positive or negative future. Self-love is useful in cultivating a foundation for ongoing forgiveness, and I will teach you how to put the past in its place and see the future as a blank canvas on which to paint an enriching life for a brighter tomorrow. We will examine case studies, ways to choose healthy relationships, means to strengthen trust, and methods to grow in a climate of personal development.

Not only can it be a challenge to accept when we are wrong, it can be a huge leap to find the power to apologize for what we have done wrong. You will come to terms with how to take this leap by harnessing empathy while putting aside your ego. Active listening goes hand in hand with this approach, and if you don't know how to be an active listener, you will learn the techniques, some through real-life examples. In addition, your ability to build bridges instead of burning them will be uncovered via the use of dialogue, discussions, mediation, and other forms of productive communication.

We will then discuss how to approach situations where you expect forgiveness, but it is not forthcoming. You will come to appreciate personal timelines, both for others and yourself, in combination with the resolve to move forward in the absence of forgiveness. Patience is a virtue that can be difficult in practice, but you will acquire the knowledge to become more patient as part of self-forgiveness, resilience, and emotional strength. Self-love and self-worth play a significant role and must be maintained to sustain a forgiving heart and a continuous willingness to learn and grow. We will talk about these endeavors and ways to set daily intentions to find peace in an environment of like-mindedness, knowledge, and empathy.

The book draws to a close by addressing your transformed life and the power that you now hold. There is a wonderful case study about how forgiveness can be used as a tool for positive social evolution, in addition to some inspirational and motivational real-life stories to emphasize the emotional peace that comes with forgiveness. The final section sets outside an exercise in self-reflection and analysis of your newfound wisdom and its role in getting rid of that pesky elephant, which becomes an appropriate note to end your journey with a view to starting a brand new one.

So, please join me, and let's dive into a set of life-changing lessons. Developing a new life that will be healthier, happier, more productive, and easier to share with those you care about.

Chapter 1

Understanding Forgiveness

If we truly understood the impact that holding onto grudges has on our mental health, we would all be motivated to practice forgiveness for our own benefit and the benefit of others. Studies have found that a whopping 69% reported lingering resentment created by a wide net of experiences, including not getting a job, being rejected in a relationship, or having a bad consumer-related experience. Although 70% acknowledged that it was harmful to their health to hold onto a grudge, about the same percentage admitted to harboring a grudge. (Sreenivasan & Weinberger, 2023).

These statistics are alarming, and the fact that such a high percentage of people are able to admit that they hold grudges despite being aware that doing so is harmful to their mental health is astounding. It also shows just how difficult it is; the assumption would be that if you knew that you would do better and grow more by forgiving, then you would forgive. But, if it were that easy, you wouldn't be reading this book and working on yourself.

Understanding Forgiveness

If we can gain a greater understanding of forgiveness, we can begin developing a culture where we practice forgiveness, with the end result of a positive impact on our mental health. Granted, grudges are very easy to develop but very hard to let go. However, we can all make a greater effort to prevent their development in the first place, and if that is not possible, we can all make a greater effort to let them go. Chances are that you are currently holding a grudge, or possibly several grudges, but I intend to change that.

Often, a grudge is a mutual feeling, and part of the block against forgiveness stems from your own inability to acknowledge that you are as much at fault as the other person. It is difficult to admit that you have done something wrong, and the easier route is to blame the person you are holding the grudge against. Even if you feel that you are one hundred percent correct, it takes a certain vulnerability to have a discussion with the other person because chances are they will point out what *you* have done wrong. This is not always the case, and a common situation where only one person is at fault is unfaithfulness in a relationship. That, however, is a discussion for later in this book, but it is possible to forgive someone in that situation without continuing the romantic relationship.

In a forgiveness situation where there is fault on the part of both individuals, it is okay to make yourself vulnerable, as this is an acceptance of partial responsibility. What follows is an apology, but it has to be genuine, and if it is, then asking for forgiveness is the next step. It may involve protracted discussion, but if both parties can get everything out and have an honest conversation, the air can be cleared, and whatever happened can remain in the past, with a lesson learned.

The Psychology Behind Grudges

Holding a grudge has its roots in psychology, and we do so in an attempt, often subconsciously, to get compassion and comfort that we feel we deserve but don't get. In these scenarios, the empathy needed is not forthcoming due to our inability to see past our impression of being wronged or unfairly treated. We focus too much on why we think we are right and ruminate on thoughts of how the other person was "wrong." The search for the comfort and compassion mentioned above becomes part of our identity, even though these notions are toxic, and that is where our mental health is adversely affected.

The self-healing comes in when we learn to love ourselves and realize that allowing the other person to have a hold over ourselves is not doing us any favors. Holding onto the pain that we have been caused is not only not detrimental to the other person but *is* detrimental to us. By placing focus on the other person, we allow them to dominate us, and from a psychological point of view, the hurt and anger are amplified.

Myths About Forgiveness

You probably know very little about forgiveness, and that is completely okay because the same goes for most people. However, if you can become aware of the myths about forgiveness, you can begin to understand it more.

Forgiveness Is About the Other Person

There is an element that has to do with the other person, as they are involved in the situation that has caused you to hold the grudge, but it is mostly about you, from the perspective that letting go of the grudge liberates *you* from the internal pain that it causes.

If You Forgive Someone, You Should Forget That It Ever Happened

Life is all about learning, and by forgetting something that was important to you at some point, you limit your ability to learn from the situation. Many people are able to forgive their former abusers but still keep the memory, and that is a good thing from the point of view of never letting it happen again and preventing it from happening to others.

Forgiveness Is a Decision

This is only a partial myth because you do have to make a conscious decision to forgive, but there is more to it than that. Along with that decision comes a commitment to actually forgive, and simply saying that you forgive someone is not enough. You have to truly stand by your decision and not just frivolously say, "I forgive you."

Refusal to Forgive Means Holding Value in Accountability

Taking accountability is a challenging task, and expecting someone else to take accountability isn't always realistic. Although it would be great for the other person to take accountability, you need to learn how to forgive in its absence, too.

Forgiveness and Reconciliation Are Not the Same Thing

Reconciliation is only possible if the other person is open to working toward achieving it. You definitely have the ability to forgive in the absence of willingness to reconcile, and when you do, it is up to the other person to be prepared to enter into discussions that will lead to reconciliation. It might seem crass to say, but once you forgive, you can't do anything further to reconcile, and that burden shifts to the other person.

The Human Tendency to Hold On to Hurt

Our brains are hardwired to favor the negative, and as a result, we tend to hold onto negative experiences, hurt being one of them. This is something that can be changed by various means, and we will talk about it as we go. As people, we have more of a proclivity to remember traumatic experiences and insults as opposed to compliments and react more strongly to negative stimuli than positive ones. This phenomenon is called the negativity bias, and it is one of the factors that make it difficult to forgive, but it can be overcome.

Emotional Anchors and Their Lasting Impact

As the name suggests, emotional anchors weigh us down, but fortunately, the ability to release ourselves from them can be learned. The effect happens when you rely solely or mostly on the first piece of information you receive or the first action of another person. If someone does something emotionally hurtful but thereafter acts with kindness and generosity, the human tendency is always to remember the first action and be unable to forgive. Your thought process could be, "People think Tony is a nice guy, and he can be, but he hurt me emotionally, so I don't see him as nice." If you were to forgive hypothetical Tony, then you are releasing the hypothetical anchor and freeing yourself from the lasting impact of that anchor. Even worse, you may write a person off completely because of one incident but dwell on the way it made you feel. I have said it before, and I will say it again, but tying that anchor to yourself and holding onto the negative emotions is not doing you any favors.

The Physiological Effects of Holding Grudges

Studies have shown that responding with anger instead of forgiveness can negatively affect one's physical health, and the likely reason is that holding grudges increases stress levels. (Toussaint, Shields, & Slavich, 2016).

Memory and perception of reality, which are not strictly physiological, can be affected by the anger and stress that are part of holding grudges. On the physical side, headaches are common, as well as insomnia and an upset stomach. In the longer term, asthma has been known to occur or worsen, and heart health can also be negatively impacted. There can be a general weakening of the immune system, which increases your risk of becoming ill and the time that it takes to recover from illness.

Resentment and Your Brain

Resentment is referred to as a tertiary emotion, which results from a secondary emotion or the combination of a primary and secondary emotion. Anger would be the primary emotion, and rage would be the secondary emotion. The reason for these allocations is that anger is an immediate emotion that is displayed at the time. It fades relatively quickly and is replaced by rage, which is a longer-lasting negative emotion. From rage comes resentment because your rage is what makes you think of the other person and how they have hurt you, i.e., what it was that made you angry. The loop of rumination over the person and the events goes over and over in your brain, and without letting go of that rumination, you will not be able to let go of your resentment either.

Mental Health Consequences of Grudges

If you have an existing mental health condition like depression and/or anxiety, holding a grudge has the potential to worsen such condition. If your mental health is generally good, developing a grudge may give you a nudge toward a full-blown mental health issue. Everything about a grudge is pessimistic, and carrying pessimism around all the time gives rise to an ongoing negative mindset. Holding a grudge can lead to isolation if the other person is part of your social circle. When a grudge causes you to withdraw because it is too painful to see the person, you are in danger of isolating yourself from the others you socialize with. So, if you are pessimistic, negative, isolated, and hold a grudge, a perfect storm of sorts is in place to dramatically affect your mental health in a negative way.

Time Heals All Wounds

Firstly, this isn't always the case, and secondly, the concept of time, or at least the *amount* of time, is subjective. If someone bumps into you by mistake in the grocery store and apologizes, chances are you realize it wasn't on purpose, and you accept the apology and move on. Two minutes into the future, and you have forgotten because it was such an innocuous event. If you were abused as a child, the pain and the memories can be so ingrained that decades can pass by before things start to get better.

Sometimes, things have to get worse before they get better. Confronting trauma is a good example. It can be exceptionally difficult, and re-living something mentally can make the hurt worse before the healing starts. You can't just rely on saying that time heals wounds while still holding onto the grudge that is keeping the wound open. It follows that forgiveness is a process, not just a one-time event, and you have to be committed to the process for your own mental well-being. You need to understand exactly how you feel about whatever happened, make a personal commitment to *want* to feel better and work through what you are feeling.

Forgiveness Versus Reconciliation

The major difference is that you can forgive someone without seeing them or talking to them. However, reconciliation involves discussion about whatever incident led to the grudge, the resentment that was created, and any other issues relating to the emotional pain associated with the situation. There is a good argument that forgiveness is easier when it is combined with reconciliation, but that may not always be the case. For reconciliation to be successful, both parties have to be prepared to reconcile, and in order to do so, you are likely to hear things from the other person that you don't like and vice-versa. Considering that, it is easy to see why there is also an argument that forgiveness is easier without reconciliation. It is, of course, very situation-dependent. It is absolutely possible to still hold a grudge against someone after they have passed away. In those circumstances, reconciliation cannot happen, but forgiveness can.

It is acceptable to be willing to forgive but not be interested in discussing anything with the other person. They don't even have to know that you have forgiven them; remember, forgiveness is for your benefit, not the benefit of the person whom you are holding a grudge against or harboring resentment toward. In the case of reconciliation, the conversation in relation thereto may not go well, and the attempt at reconciliation could fail. You could walk away from that situation, accept that reconciliation just isn't possible, but still forgive the other person. Probably the best outcome is reconciliation and forgiveness, but if only forgiveness is possible, you are still making really good ground for your mental well-being.

Setting Boundaries

Anger, frustration, resentment, and grudges result from some boundaries being crossed. If you are walking with your phone in your hand, and someone snatches it and runs off, a personal boundary has been crossed. You are completely justified to feel all sorts of negative emotions toward the thief. The hope would always be that this wouldn't happen, but if it does, forgiveness is easier, more often than not, because you have no emotional connection with the person. However, if someone close to you crosses a boundary, and as a result, you are hurt emotionally, forgiveness will probably be more difficult than in the stolen cell phone situation. The thing with relationships is that you need to make boundaries patently clear from the outset. If you know what the other person's boundaries are, and they know what yours are, then there should be enough mutual respect to remain within the boundaries. Cheating on your partner would be an example of a crossed boundary. Betraying a friend in any way would also cross a boundary, and breaking someone's trust by telling someone else something that was shared with you in confidence is another example of boundary crossing.

Safety Versus Opening Old Wounds

If there is any form of trauma from your past, you may be consciously or even subconsciously trying to put a band-aid over it to keep it from causing further trauma. If this is the case, you are not actually repairing the wound, just compartmentalizing it as a safe option. The wound needs stitches, so you are not really keeping it safe because it is still there, and it exists. If you peel the band-aid back and begin to stitch the wound slowly, you can repair it and let it heal. The scar that will remain is the memory, but the wound is no longer there. Serious trauma that you have been holding onto for years or even decades is not going to disappear immediately. You have to go through the entire forgiveness process, and we are going to go into much greater detail in that regard later in the book. Deep-seated trauma is best addressed with a therapist, but you can also work at it on your own, outside of your therapy sessions. To sum up, you may think that you are being safe by using the band-aid, but in reality, you are just masking the pain, which still remains present.

Chapter Summary

Statistically, about 70% of people hold grudges, half of which are aware that doing so is harmful. To change these numbers, you need to understand forgiveness, specifically, the fact that by avoiding forgiveness, you are only hurting yourself. The major myth about forgiving is that it is for the other person's benefit. Further myths include the idea that after forgiveness, you should forget and that refusing to forgive means that you value accountability that is not forthcoming from the other person. Emotional anchors weigh us down, and holding onto grudges can have physical implications, too. Forgiveness can accompany reconciliation, but it doesn't have to. Setting boundaries early on in any relationship can prevent, or at the least assist in preventing, occurrences that may lead to anger, frustration, and resentment. Finally, you can't just throw a band-aid on wounds from past trauma; you need to stitch them up to properly repair the situation and have the scar as a reminder that no longer evokes the trauma.

We are about to transition into the next chapter, which begins with a powerful story of how refusing to forgive tore apart a relationship, followed by an analysis of just how heavy the weight of "unforgiveness" can be.

Chapter 2:

The Heaviness of

"Unforgiveness"

The true story that follows happened in 2014, and resentment is still present as of the time of writing. For anonymity, the names of the people involved have been changed.

James and his girlfriend Carin shared a house with a very close friend of theirs, Barry, whose half-brother Brian would often visit. One night, the four friends went out drinking. James decided to drive, which was very irresponsible but isn't actually relevant to the story. However, I would like to emphasize that you should *never* drink and drive.

At some point in the evening, Barry and Brian had a disagreement. They were causing a scene in the bar that the four were at, and as a result, the manager asked Barry and Brian to leave. James and Carin decided to stay at the bar despite Barry and Brian asking them to leave together. On the way out, Brian took James' car keys from Carin's handbag without her noticing, and he and Barry took James' car home.

Barry and Brian, screaming and shouting at each other, arrived home. While driving through the gates, Brian managed to scrape James' car on a wall. The two half-brothers started pushing and shoving each other, and soon enough, the punches started flying. Eventually, things calmed down, although Barry had a large cut just above his eye. Both brothers lay down and ended up passing out.

During this time, James and Carin had decided that it was time to go home, but to their horror, James' car was gone. They immediately thought the car had been stolen, so they were forced to take a taxi home. Needless to say, the couple was not prepared for the scene that greeted them. James shook Barry violently, then moved onto Brian, and a shouting match ensued when the two men woke up. James screamed at them to leave while Carin stood there dumbfounded. Barry pleaded with James to let him into the house so that he could clean his wound, but to no avail. Brian then convinced Barry that it would be best to leave and re-address the issue in the morning.

The half-brothers spent the rest of the night in a nearby park, and when they woke up, they walked back to the house. Much to their surprise, all of Barry's belongings were sitting on the front lawn with a note that told Barry that he would not be let back in and that he needed to find somewhere else to live. He tried to phone James, who didn't answer; the same was true with Carin. Fortunately, Barry and Brian had patched things up, and Brian invited Barry to stay with him until Barry could find another place to live.

The half-brothers called a taxi and went back to Brian's house so that they could get his car to go back and collect Barry's belongings. When they returned to Brian's house, they tried to contact James and Carin, but neither answered their calls or replied to their text messages.

To cut a long story short, nine years have passed, and James and Carin have not spoken to Barry despite his requests to meet and talk about what happened. Barry and Brian have conveyed their apologies over text and email. They harbor no guilt or resentment and are both very willing to patch up the relationship. However, James and Carin both hold grudges, and the toxic effect that the grudges have on them is very noticeable. Every so often, Carin suggests that the couple should contact Barry and Brian, but James is completely unwilling to do so.

The sad thing is that Barry and Brian have long let go of what happened, and one may argue that it is easier for them because they are more at fault. The half-brothers hold no resentment and no emotional pain, but James and Carin are the complete opposite. Who do you think is worse off in the situation? Yes, I know your answer is James and Carin, and I know that you can see that they are the figurative poison drinkers. I also know that you will take away a lesson from this story. So, let's carry on, and I will arm you with more knowledge and tips to avoid being a James or a Carin.

The Stress Connection

To expand on how stress and resentment are linked, it is the latter that induces stress because of the negative emotions associated. You may experience the "lump in the throat" feeling, and when stress gets really bad, it can actually feel like something is stuck in your throat permanently. If you have worries that are unrelated to resentment, you may start thinking about that resentment on top of your worrying because of the general negative connotations. The mental health impact is obviously significant, but stress manifests physically in the form of headaches, high blood pressure, poor libido, shaking, and dizziness, amongst other ailments.

The Mental Haze

Forgiveness and Depression

Firstly, let me explain the difference between clinical and circumstantial depression, and then we will talk about the impact that forgiveness or lack thereof can have on depression. Clinical depression refers to what people loosely refer to as a chemical imbalance where there is an issue with the production of serotonin in the brain. Circumstantial depression is when an event causes extreme sadness that can be accompanied by a number of other emotions. For instance, if you lose your job or a loved one passes away, you may find yourself sliding into depression. Resentment can have the same effect. Let's use divorce as an example. You may harbor anger and resentment toward your partner during and after the divorce. The feelings that you feel and the grudge that you won't let go can be big contributing factors to depression. If you already struggle with clinical depression, resentment and grudges can make the situation worse. Then, you have depression as a result of asking for forgiveness without any success. This is the other side of resentment and is linked to guilt. If you are genuinely sorry and remorseful, there will be guilt involved, too. Being forgiven is one of the factors that can alleviate your guilt, and if you reach out to someone you have hurt but they are not interested in talking to you, the guilt can lead to or worsen depression.

Resentment, Cognition, the Rumination Loop, and a Peaceful Mind

We all have cognitive abilities, and these include being able to acquire knowledge and retain it. Our cognition is also responsible for memory, logic, and the way we perceive concepts. As you age, your cognition declines, and this is only natural. Sometimes, the decline is hardly noticeable; your memory may worsen slightly, and it could take you longer to understand new concepts. On the other end of the spectrum, cognitive decline can be so extreme that it manifests as Alzheimer's or dementia. Resentment has the potential to accelerate cognitive decline, and although this may be a "future you" problem, it is just another reason to practice forgiveness. The continuous thoughts of and dwelling on what you are resentful for and who you are resentful toward is known as the rumination loop, which can impair thinking, contribute to poor decision-making, and lead to impulsivity.

We all want peace of mind, but the truth is that very few people actually find it. Resentment is a huge impediment to peace of mind, even though your soul may yearn for it. I am going to leave a bullet point list that stipulates what can be done to work toward peace of mind, and we will expand on those points in Chapter Four.

- accept the things in your life that you cannot control

- forgive yourself and others

- focus on the present (mindfulness comes into this one)

- journaling

- meditation and looking within

Repairing a Relationship

You have to decide whether you *want* to repair a relationship. If you think back to James and Carin and Barry and Brian, the latter two want to repair the relationship but hold no resentment toward the former two or themselves. James and Carin still hold resentment and are not interested in repairing the relationship. Even though Barry and Brian would like to repair the relationship, they will not be psychologically affected if it doesn't happen. James and Carin will have to be the ones to reach out in order to start taking steps to repair the relationship, and that would be the best thing for them to do for their own mental well-being. Let's look at what all four parties would have to do in order to repair the relationship.

Take Full Responsibility

Barry and Brian have already taken responsibility because they have forgiven themselves. The half-brothers know that they are at fault and would love to have the chance to offer their apologies to James and Carin. They have also completely forgiven James and Carin for putting Barry's belongings outside the house. James and Carin have yet to take responsibility for their actions, which they would have to do in order to start repairing the relationship.

Show Care and Compassion

To extend the example, Barry and Brian are prepared to be caring and compassionate, whereas James and Carin are not. In fact, they can't be because they are unwilling to take responsibility for *their* actions.

Have an Open and Honest Conversation

During these discussions, the full responsibility part, as well as care and compassion, would be talked about and displayed. Ideally, Barry and Brian would get across exactly what happened to cause their disagreement, why they took James' car without asking, and details about everything else that transpired. James and Carin would have to convey that they have taken responsibility for putting Barry's belongings outside and explain how they understand that creating the situation was not the right way to go about things. If the couple is genuine, then the care and compassion would be evident.

The Decision

Depending on how the conversation goes, all parties may want to revive the relationship. Alternatively, the parties may want to shake hands or exchange hugs, knowing that the relationship has been repaired but also in agreement that they will continue to lead separate lives. Although one would hope that the relationship would be repaired and restored, the main and most important part is that forgiveness is present in everyone involved and that they have all let go of grudges and resentment.

"Unforgiveness" and Spirituality

The concept of spirituality is quite a broad one and also one that differs from person to person. The basic idea is that there is something bigger than ourselves in operation. Some people find spirituality in religion or in the form of a supernatural being. Others feel a connection with the universe, and there is also the belief that spirituality flows from person to person. It is a very individual connection in the pursuit of inner peace. As you can imagine, being unable to forgive either other people or yourself is almost guaranteed to get in the way of developing a spiritual connection. Having said that, exploring spirituality can assist in the process of forgiveness because that exploration could lead to the realization that "unforgiveness" does indeed get in the way of that. If you are struggling to forgive, it may be worthwhile to explore spirituality by doing some research, attending a spiritual retreat, or easing into it through a therapist. The benefits may include the following:

- develop a sense of purpose and meaning

- o Some people question what life is all about, and others just get on with it. The world's greatest questions are as follows:

  - Where did we come from?

  - Why are we here?

  - Where are we going?

- o You could also throw in, "What is the point of it all?" In any event, these great questions may be subject to some great answers through spirituality, and even if answers are not forthcoming, you could develop your own individual purpose and draw meaning from something personal to you.

- cope with stress, depression, and anxiety

- give you optimism, hope, and a restored semblance of hope in humanity

- the feeling that you are part of something bigger

Spirituality has proven instrumental in stress management and coping with negativity. It also explores what it means to be human, including both good and bad. Gratitude is also synonymous with spirituality, and keeping a gratitude journal is something that you can implement before you even look into spirituality. The way that it works is by writing down everything that you are grateful for in your life, which would include your interpersonal relationships with family and friends. Keeping a gratitude journal could help you realize what is important in life and put the emotional harm of "unforgiveness" into perspective. Other aspects of spirituality might do the same thing, and if so, the ability to forgive and how you put it into practice will positively affect your overall well-being...and that...is...what...you...want!

"Unforgiveness" and Trust

If you have had your trust broken in the past, and as a result, you have been unable to forgive, you may struggle to trust people in the future. It is a case of once bitten, twice shy, but if you can restore trust after the first bite, you have a greater chance of trusting as time goes by. Alternatively, forgiving someone for breaking your trust can repair the negative associations and, by so doing, also repair your trust for the other person.

If you have been hurt in a romantic relationship, and as a result, it comes to an end, there is a strong possibility that you will struggle to trust a future romantic partner, and such lack of trust could look something like the following:

- always assuming the worst

- being suspicious about your partner's intentions

- self-sabotage

- creating a divide between yourself and your partner

- struggling to commit fully to the relationship

The situation would be exactly the same when your partner breaks your trust, and you remain in the relationship. The forgiveness process has to take place before trust can be regained. There is a possibility of forgiving but still leaving the relationship if the breach of trust was to such an extent that a continued relationship is no longer viable. The bottom line is that practicing "unforgiveness" will not repair trust but will cause continued emotional pain.

"Unforgiveness" and Personal Growth

We talked about emotional anchors in the previous chapter, and being tied down by one means that forward motion is difficult to harness. It goes without saying that to grow, we need to move forward, and practicing "unforgiveness" is very limiting in that regard. Without personal growth, we don't improve as human beings, and a major part of the lack of improvement is rooted in the unwillingness to forgive.

By forgiving, you open a path to personal growth because the angry or resentful thoughts are no longer the ones that are dominant. You also remove yourself from victim mode, which ties in with your emphasis on accountability that the other person has not shown. You actually stop caring that you may have been a victim or that the other person won't take accountability. Forgiving gives you a sense of freedom and transfers the energy you were spending negatively onto the other person to energy that you can spend on bettering yourself, moving forward, and growing as a person.

Chapter Summary

I'm not going to address the whole story of James, Carin, Brian, and Barry, but I urge you to take away the important point that Brian and Barry are in a much better emotional place than James and Carin. The reason for this is due to the half-brothers being able to forgive the couple and themselves, thus breaking free from resentment.

You can get stuck in a mental haze when you refuse to forgive, and depression can be a result, whether circumstantial or clinical, with circumstantial considerations that amplify the depression. As we age, our cognitive abilities decline, but resentment can accelerate that decline by forming a constant loop of rumination and robbing you of peace of mind.

In order to repair a relationship, you need to take responsibility, be caring and compassionate, have honest conversations, and, when you are finished, decide whether to forgive and walk away or forgive and move forward with the relationship. There is a spirituality element, and whether you find your spirituality through a higher being, emotional connections, or anything else, being unable to forgive places a huge block on attaining the level of spirituality that you otherwise would. Trust and personal growth are other areas that "unforgiveness" impacts. It is difficult to regain trust, and forgiving is essential to do so. In addition, personal growth can be kickstarted through forgiveness.

Just by reading the above summary and thinking about the content prior thereto, I am sure that you have realized or are beginning to realize just how damaging grudge-holding can be. These realizations and a commitment to action can bring about healing, so please join me as we address everything healing-related in the next chapter.

Chapter 3:

The Healing Journey Begins

In order for the light to shine so brightly, the darkness must be present. –
Francis Bacon

We humans love the juxtaposition between day and night, representing good and bad, as well as light and dark, taking on the same representations; just look at music, literature, and poetry. It thus seems fitting to use a Francis Bacon quote to open this chapter (Aydin, n.d.).

You may not have heard of Francis Bacon, but I can describe him in two ways. Firstly, an old guy who dressed funny, and secondly, a lawyer, philosopher, and essayist born in the United Kingdom in 1561. (At the time, everyone dressed in a way that we find funny today).

The quote is so simple, yet so powerful, and it offers comfort in the fact that life comes with darkness, but light is attainable, whether the darkness is anger, resentment, hate, or a combination of all three in the form of a grudge.

Before healing can begin, you need to accept that you are experiencing resentment. If you don't acknowledge it, then in your mind, you don't believe that you are resentful or that you hold a grudge, even though, deep down, if you are absolutely honest with yourself, you *will* know. In any event, it is well worth exploring some signs that are resentment indicators.

- unfounded anger, and getting angry in unprompted outbursts

- being petty and sweating the small things

- you harbor desperation to make the other person aware of how you feel

- pushing responsibility for your feelings onto others

- you have no self-compassion

- you talk badly about the other person behind their back

- a refusal to look at the situation from other perspectives

You should also value feedback from family and friends and explore therapy, but before we get there, I would like to expand on vulnerability.

Vulnerability, Forgiveness, and Growth

Being vulnerable may not be associated with strength in your mind, but there could be more to it than you think. Although being vulnerable exposes weaknesses, it can be used to build strength. Take the example of telling your romantic partner that you love them for the first time. That is an act of vulnerability, based on the possibility that your partner may not say it back. The inner strength stems from the resilience that builds up, but that is not to say that your partner doesn't love you; perhaps they are just not ready to say it yet. This is probably the most common example of what vulnerability involves, but in a situation where there has been mutual hurt and where mutual forgiveness is sought, vulnerability operates on a different level. Firstly, there is admitting that you were wrong, apologizing, asking for forgiveness, and having the difficult conversations that will follow. Many people avoid opening themselves up to vulnerability for fear of being hurt or hurting others.

To keep the theme of forgiveness running, let's say that you have done something to upset a friend. Perhaps you have talked about them behind their back to another person. That other person has then told your friend, and as a result, you are feeling regret and anger toward yourself, in addition to anger directed at the person whom you talked to about your friend. You realize that had you not talked badly about your friend, you wouldn't have self-directed anger, nor would you have anger directed at the person who you talked to *about* your friend.

Firstly, you would have to be honest with yourself and admit that your actions were wrong. Secondly, you need to be genuinely remorseful. Your next move is to plan a conversation with your friend, during which you plan to apologize. Because of the anger that your friend probably feels toward you, there is a chance that he or she will tell you exactly how they feel about you based on your breach of trust. Generally, we don't like to hear negative things about our personality and disposition, which is why your prospective apology makes you emotionally vulnerable. Just the act of asking for forgiveness is one of vulnerability due to the possibility that forgiveness will not be forthcoming.

There is another element to the situation, in that in your eyes, you may be angry with the other person, but you have no right to be. You actually owe them an apology because of breaking your friend's trust and putting the other person in the awkward position of having to decide whether or not to tell your friend about the breach of trust. Addressing the situation with that person once again puts you in a vulnerable state.

Unfortunately, in the example above, the damage that has been caused cannot be blamed on anyone else. Perhaps you can use this example as a lesson, which will prevent you from causing emotional hurt to others and yourself.

When vulnerability brings on forgiveness, whether you are forgiving or being forgiving, it gives you a chance to grow as an individual and a chance for your relationship to grow. There is a huge trust element to vulnerability. Giving someone the opportunity to hurt you emotionally but hoping that they won't is brave. By doing so, you make yourself very vulnerable, and if the other person does not hurt you emotionally as a result of your vulnerability, you learn that they can be trusted, which is a cornerstone of any relationship.

Making yourself vulnerable also teaches you to become better at expressing yourself emotionally and, thus, growing from an emotional perspective. This applies not only to holding grudges or refusing to forgive but also in a holistic sense. It does, however, also help you to understand forgiveness because of your emotional enlightenment. To bring some practicality to the hypothetical examples, I would like to spend some time addressing how to incorporate vulnerability into your life.

Resolve to Embrace Vulnerability

Don't consider your reluctance to be vulnerable as a weakness, but do consider your desire to allow yourself to put yourself in vulnerable situations as a strength. If you take a resolution to embrace vulnerability, it is a bit like a "face your fear" gambit. I want to make it clear that vulnerability is not necessarily the fear. The possible result of vulnerability is a fear, which differs from person to person and from situation to situation.

Understand Vulnerability

It is safe to say that the contents of this chapter so far have improved your understanding of vulnerability, but I would like to briefly clarify. It includes willingness to make mistakes, being big enough to apologize, and the ability to participate in difficult conversations where there is a possibility of negative emotional outcomes. Obviously, we always *hope* for positive outcomes, and if they were guaranteed, vulnerability wouldn't exist.

Recognize the Benefits

Being honest is difficult, but it creates fewer complications and offers up the potential to grow and develop deeper emotional connections. With benefits like these, you can see how embracing vulnerability can greatly serve you and others in your life.

Self-Awareness and Compassion

If you show someone else your vulnerabilities, and they show you theirs, there is mutual compassion, which comes from greater self-awareness. Exposing your emotional self allows you to be more aware of yourself as a person and often requires introspective thought.

Step Outside Your Comfort Zone

Fear of rejection, which can be part of being hurt emotionally, is something that keeps many people from stepping out of their comfort zones. However, it is when we become uncomfortable that we learn, grow, and expand our comfort zones. Hiding our vulnerability is akin to remaining in a comfort zone, and displaying our vulnerability is akin to stepping outside it.

Myths About Vulnerability

Arguably, the foremost myth is that vulnerability is equal to weakness, but if you think about it, we generally value honesty on the part of others, but we can be reluctant to give back the same thing. Absolute honesty makes us vulnerable, but not weak, and we shouldn't associate vulnerability with emotional weakness; in fact, letting your vulnerability show is courageous. In many scenarios, you are putting yourself out there, and that takes bravery. There is another myth that not everyone experiences vulnerability. Perhaps fully-fledged psychopaths are the exception, but the rest of us have bouts of emotional uncertainty and the risks that come along with it. Individuals who believe they are not vulnerable are merely hiding their emotional uncertainty, arguably subconsciously, but vulnerability is *still* present, just not on display.

Vulnerability is not equal to sharing our secrets with the world or with anyone for that matter. There are some parts of ourselves that only the people closest to us will ever know about, and that is completely acceptable. You don't need to reveal your insecurities or fears to everyone you meet. You are the one in charge of who gets to know what about you. Not discussing the things that make you vulnerable with everyone that you meet is not dishonesty, and it is your right to discuss those things with whoever you choose to. Furthermore, we don't have to be vulnerable all the time, in the same way that we don't feel other emotions on a constant basis. You aren't happy all the time, sad all the time, or excited all the time, so logically, you are not vulnerable all the time.

The Path to Emotional Healing

As you know, harboring resentment and holding grudges don't pave the way to emotional healing. You are also aware that forgiveness is not just saying "I'm sorry," but it is an ongoing process that leads the way to emotional healing. But how do you know that you are healing emotionally?

Allowing Yourself to Feel Your Emotions

Not every emotion is negative, but we most often focus on the negative ones. When you hold anger, *you* may think that it is not having an effect on you, but in reality, you are just suppressing it. Because it is still present, you need to allow yourself to feel it without judgment, and only then can you begin to heal emotionally, which incorporates forgiveness. You need to allow yourself to feel all of your emotions, including the positive ones, so don't forget about them!

Emotional Clarity

You start to become clearer on how you feel your emotions and what feelings act as triggers, good or bad. Once this stage is reached, you will get better at setting boundaries that protect your emotions where they need protecting. Having been hurt in the past, you may not be the best at prioritizing your own well-being, but when your emotional outlook is clearer, focusing on yourself as a priority becomes easier.

Responding Rather Than Reacting

Reacting without thinking, getting frustrated too soon, and displaying anger as a result of small triggers are synonymous with holding onto emotional pain. If you are able to pause, absorb what has been said or done, and respond calmly, you are more in control of your emotions, which is a sign that you are progressing well along the healing path.

Trusting the Process

Like anyone, you will have good and bad days. Sometimes, you may think that you are not progressing, but it is incumbent on you to realize that emotional healing is not linear and that there will be ups and downs.

Acknowledging Disappointments

Holding onto hurt is often accompanied by a "why me?" attitude, which involves questioning every disappointment and feeling like you can never win and the world keeps knocking you down. This is, of course, not the case. Life comes with setbacks, and so does the healing process. Learning to recognize that disappointments happen to billions of people every single day should provide some form of emotional comfort and allow you to acknowledge them for what they are before pushing on.

You Welcome Support

The mentality that you can heal on your own may look strong on the surface, but when the people in your life want to help and support you, they may assist in a faster healing process.

Therapy

Therapy is also a form of support that you should be open to welcoming into your life when you want to embark on the forgiveness road. There is a stigma attached to therapy, and a school of thought that you are weak if you seek out therapy.

This is so far from the truth, and besides, if you are looking for emotional help and assistance in forgiving, and it works, then it doesn't matter what other people think. You need to prioritize yourself (reminder).

If you do seek out therapy after reading this book, your understanding of anger, resentment, grudge-holding, and forgiveness will allow you to make faster progress with your therapist. Perhaps you will need only a few sessions, but you may want to make therapy a regular thing. Let's take a look at three of the more popular techniques when it comes to forgiveness therapy.

Enright Model

This technique of forgiveness therapy was developed by educational psychologist Robert Enright and consists of four phases.

Phase One: Uncovering

The therapist will take you through the way in which your psychological defenses work. This allows you to identify the negative feelings and emotions that you are experiencing and evaluate the psychological harm associated therewith.

Phase Two: Decision Making

You and your therapist will discuss the possibility of forgiveness and reach a conscious decision that you are ready to start the process.

Phase Three: Cognitive Reframing

Your therapist will guide you along a path of developing empathy for the person that you have anger and resentment toward, and accept the pain experienced.

Phase Four: Deepening

You will be helped to find a deeper meaning in your suffering in a way that can benefit you going forward as you release the pain but remember the cause behind it.

The REACH Model

This model splits forgiveness into five chronological steps, as follows:

(R)ecall the Emotional Hurt

You will be prompted to talk about everything involving the hurt that you felt and still feel, including the incident or incidents that are responsible for the hurt. This might be a painful process, as you will probably mentally relive the past, which can have a significant emotional impact.

(E)mpathy For the Offender

This is done in a similar manner to phase three in the Enright Model.

Forgiveness as an (A)ltruistic Gift for the Offender

You can summarize this step as a gesture of unselfish forgiveness, with no expectation of anything in return; hence it is altruistic in nature.

(C)ommitment to Forgive

As I have said before, saying "I forgive you" isn't enough. You need to be fully committed and prepared to walk the necessary path.

(H)olding on to Forgiveness

This takes the commitment step one further, and you need to keep the forgiveness alive and not let go of it and slip back into anger and resentment.

Forgiveness Letter

Sitting down and writing a letter of forgiveness can be incredibly therapeutic. Your therapist may ask you to do this as homework for the two of you to analyze in the next session. It is important to get everything out, and this is something that you do right now. If you would like to give it a try, I suggest you use the two previous models as guidance.

Your therapist may use a combination of these models, but remember that emotional pain is experienced differently, and a good therapist will embark on a treatment program that is tailored to your specific situation.

Support Groups

Sharing your story with other people can be very freeing, and sometimes, it is actually easier to open up to strangers than people close to you. Group therapy can be useful in understanding your emotional hurt when compared to others. There will no doubt be similarities but also differences, and the possibility of connecting with people who have experienced trauma on a level that you may not be able to with others is something that you should explore.

Outside Sources

This book could be considered an outside source, and I encourage you to explore other literature about forgiveness. Self-help books, articles, and blogs are excellent for your general well-being. Reading inspirational quotes or stories, watching inspirational documentaries, and listening to inspirational podcasts are all ways to inspire positivity, which goes a long way when addressing your anger, resentment, and/or grudge-holding.

Chapter Summary

Forgiveness has to be followed by acceptance that you are resentful. Indicators of resentment, among others, are unprompted outbursts, being petty, and a lack of self-compassion. There is a certain amount of vulnerability when it comes to forgiveness, and the positive element of vulnerability is personal growth. Don't forget that vulnerability is not a sign of weakness but rather an act of strength along the path of emotional healing. In order to heal properly, you need to allow yourself to feel your emotions, acknowledge disappointments, and welcome support. One form of support is therapy, and I refer you back to the three methods discussed. Support groups and other sources, such as literature and inspirational material, can improve your mental well-being. The ultimate result will be letting go, and to that end, it is time to dig deeper into letting go in the next chapter.

Chapter 4:

The Mechanics of Letting Go

Think back once again to the alarming statistic in Chapter 1. To remind you, Although 70% of people know that it is harmful to their health to hold onto a grudge, about the same percentage admit to holding one. (Sreenivasan & Weinberger, 2023).

This just shows how difficult it is to let go, and if we don't know the intricacies of what it means to let go, it may never happen. Fortunately, you are in good hands and are about to learn everything you need to know on the subject.

Introspection and Journaling

Looking within yourself and focusing on your feelings and emotions is an exercise in introspection. It requires honesty and can be accomplished effectively when done in conjunction with journaling. Writing things down makes them more real, and you can look at it as a way to record your inward experiences in a way that creates progress toward letting go. What follows is a list of suggested prompts that you can follow in order to be introspective and record the results of your introspection in writing.

- the source of resentment

  - You may think that you know the source of your resentment, and of course, you do, to an extent, but here you have the chance to really analyze that source. Think about any sights, smells, and physical feelings associated with the source, revisit the details of exactly what happened, describe the people involved, and be as specific as you can.

- write down all your emotions

  - Make a list, and expand on the different emotions, whether they are sadness, anger, frustration, resentment, etc. Take some time to go into the details of how these emotions are impacting your life.

- identify any beliefs that are responsible for placing limitations on you.

  - If past trauma has resulted in beliefs that you are not good enough, that you are destined for failure, or that you always disappoint people, you need to write them all down and acknowledge that they are limiting in nature.

- consider the bigger picture

    o Ask yourself, in written form, if continuing to hold onto emotional pain is of use in the bigger picture. The answer is definitely no! So write it down, and follow up with a list of reasons explaining the bigger picture and the relative insignificance of resentment and not letting go.

The idea is not to do this once but to journal on a regular basis so that you can remind yourself that letting go is beneficial to you. The more you journal, the less prominent the effect of your negative emotions will become as you get better at letting go, even if the process takes place through small steps.

Mindfulness and Letting Go

The major focus of mindfulness is the *focus*. That is, paying acute attention to the present and remaining in the moment. Resentment and all the emotions and feelings accompanying it can contribute to the negative rumination loop we discussed in the previous chapter. Mindfulness can be a great tool to distract ourselves from the negativity caused by resentment, as an exercise to supplement our conscious efforts to let go. If you can focus on the present and immerse yourself in the moment, you are able to distract yourself from the thoughts that accompany resentment. By doing so, you spend less time on being resentful, and less time spent on being resentful is of great assistance in letting go.

One of the great things about mindfulness is that you can practice it just about anywhere and just about at any time. As I said, the premise is acute focus, so let's take eating a meal as an example. Doing so mindfully involves paying attention to each bite, including the texture, the smell, and the taste, from the point it touches your lips, the way that you slowly chew, how the flavors explode in your mouth, to the feeling as you swallow, before taking the next bite. When you are completely absorbed in the experience of eating a meal, there isn't any time for resentment. This doesn't necessarily mean that you have suddenly let go of your resentment, but you have paid no attention to it during your mindful meal. Because you are human, there is no doubt that thoughts will enter your mind and distract your focus from the smells, textures, and tastes. This is completely normal, but knowing that it will happen gives you the capacity to identify intrusive thoughts, stop them in their tracks, dismiss them, and re-align your focus to what you are doing at that present moment.

Now, think about your day from when you wake up in the morning to when you go to bed at night. There are a lot of seemingly mundane things that happen. In the context of mindfulness, you can take the mundanity out of them and occupy your mind, thus staving off thoughts of resentment and negativity in general. Perhaps you have coffee in bed in the morning. If so, clear your mind and focus on each sip in a similar way to mindful eating. When you shower, enjoy the experience of the warm droplets hitting your back and head, then running down your body before pooling and flowing down the drain. On your way to work, observe your surroundings and appreciate the beauty of what you see. Pay close attention to the sights, sounds, smells, textures, and any other observable experiences.

You get the idea. Mindfulness isn't specifically directed at letting go of emotional pain, but it greatly assists in creating the kind of focus that distracts from the emotional pain. Logically, the less time you spend on negative emotions, including resentment, the less you *experience* the negative effects of those emotions. At the end of the day, mindfulness, as we have just discussed, is a supplementary factor that contributes to the overall pursuit of letting go.

Meditation

There is a large part of mindfulness that deals with meditation, so meditation could have been included in the above section, but I would like to address it separately. One of the tenets of meditation, in the same vein as mindfulness, is to focus on the present. Meditation is not only for monks; you can find guided meditations on many platforms, including Spotify, Apple Music, and YouTube. The premise is similar to mindfulness in that while focusing on the present, your attention is not on anger, resentment, or the like, and thus, you are spending less time involving your thoughts in negativity. Let's take a look at an example of meditation directed specifically at forgiveness.

1. Sit in a comfortable position, close your eyes, and focus on your breathing. Take a deep breath through your nose. Hold for a moment, and release slowly through your mouth. You should notice your heart rate slowing down as you focus on your chest rising and falling.

2. In your mind's eye, picture the person who has hurt you and who is responsible for the emotional pain that you feel.

3. Name the emotions that the vision of this person evokes, for example, embarrassment, shame, anger, hate, or the like.

4. Pause for a moment and examine your physical state. You should be aiming for relaxation, but if you feel

tense or stressed, switch focus back to your breathing until you feel your heart rate slowing down again.

5. Then evoke the thought of the person who has hurt you, and come up with a phrase that you can repeat, such as, "I have no anger toward you. I forgive you and wish you love and happiness."

6. Try to visualize the resentment leaving your body. It may be in the form of a ton of bricks or something more abstract; whatever works best for you.

Before we continue, I would like to tell you the story of a woman named Mary Hedges, who was able to let go of resentment as a result of forgiveness meditation. Mary was at a mall with her son when she was hit by a shopping cart that was pushed off a railing on a higher level. Her injuries were severe, including brain damage, blindness in one eye, and an amputated right foot. Mary underwent therapy, which was largely meditation-centered, and managed to completely let go of any resentment. In an interview with ABC News, Mary, when talking about the boys that had pushed the cart, said, "I wish them well, I do. My son is 13 also, and he is a very good boy" (LaBianca, 2022).

It is truly incredible that someone can suffer so incredibly and still find the power to let go and forgive, which is a testament to how powerful forgiveness meditation can be.

Expressive Therapy as an Outlet

We express ourselves through language, and part of that is body language, but in terms of releasing emotional pain, we can look to other forms of expression in the creative realm.

Perhaps you are thinking that you are not artistic or musical. Don't worry; you don't have to be, but you are on the right track with your thinking.

- art therapy

    o By occupying your mind with drawing, painting, or sculpting, you can escape from emotional pain by transferring it into the art that you are busy creating. You don't have to be particularly good, as the point is not just the art but letting go of your anger and resentment by using art as your outlet.

- dance therapy

    o Physical movement is a good way to let go expressively and cope with emotions that threaten your mental well-being.

- music therapy

    o Everyone knows that music can be powerful on an emotional level, and thus, using it to express yourself in the pursuit of letting go can be particularly effective.

- writing therapy

    o You know about this one already, in the form of journaling, which has also proven to be instrumental in letting go.

It is definitely worth looking into expressive therapy. Many therapists in this field will offer a free session so you can get an idea if you think it will work for you.

Exercise

Physical activity has many benefits, and aside from the obvious, i.e., health and fitness, exercise can be used as a means to forgive. Firstly, exercise is a natural antidepressant because of the dopamine effect. Dopamine, loosely known as "the happy hormone," is released during physical activity and is an automatic mood lifter that improves your general state of mind. By exercising and then cooling down with a meditation session, concentration is heightened, and the mind is more alert, which means that your ability to meditate is enhanced. The knock-on effect is a faster path to letting go.

Physical activity can double as a form of mindfulness, and depending on the intensity of your exercise session, you can go through the steps of the forgiveness meditation detailed above. Please keep your eyes open, though. A form of exercise that involves a mental aspect is a gratitude run/jog. Basically, you set out on a slow run or jog, and as you go, you list all the things you are grateful for in your life, similar to how you would do while journaling. The idea is to gain perspective and start to understand that there are too many good things in your life to allow emotional pain to weigh you down. It facilitates an alternative way of thinking, and the positivity that it produces can be carried through to your other letting-go activities.

Nature and Emotional Healing

Just being in nature can be a healing experience, and noticing the harmony of the natural world has the potential to show us that we are insignificant in the greater scheme of things. Not in the sense that we don't matter and that our interpersonal relationships don't matter, but in the sense that nature existed before we did, and it will exist after we no longer do. Going on a hike, a walk in a forest, or just sitting in a park and observing your surroundings are good exercises for the should, and that is where the healing begins.

When your mind aligns with nature, it can feel like everything slows down, including your thoughts, which leads to an overall calmness and clearer thought patterns. Being in nature ties in with mindfulness, as there are so many sensory elements to nature that you can focus on. The whole experience is directed at the realization that letting go will serve us best from an emotional growth point of view.

I am not saying that one walk through a forest is going to heal all your emotional pain and make you instantly let go. However, regular encounters with nature can supplement all your other methods of coming to terms with your emotions, working toward forgiveness, and ultimately reaching your goal of letting go.

The Difficult Questions

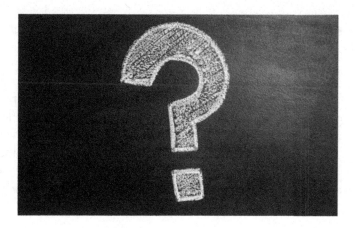

You will have noticed that this chapter has dealt with thought, focus on the present, and self-talk, or at least visualization of emotions and feelings. I would like to add to that with a set of questions that you can ask yourself and then answer to gain a persona and understanding of your specific resentment, from which point implementing the specifics of this chapter becomes ever so slightly easier...remember, letting go is not a quick process.

- Where does my resentment come from?

    o This may not be an easy question to answer because you may have an idea of where it comes from but haven't addressed it fully. When you answer this question try to be very specific and think of every emotion and feeling on your own, one by one.

- If my resentment could speak, what would it say?

    o This is quite an abstract question, and it allows you free reign to give your resentment a voice. Imagine a back-and-forth conversation between yourself and your resentment, in which you ask it questions and answer on its behalf.

- If I had to choose, what would I want to happen to resolve my resentment?

    o You may want the other person to feel emotional pain or for something bad to happen to them. This is only natural, so don't judge yourself if you answer the question in a mean-spirited way. As I have said, you are following a process, and getting the truth about how you feel out in the open is a step to changing the way you feel.

- Is it possible to forgive?

  - The answer to this question has to be "yes." The time may not have arrived yet, but you need to keep the possibility open. If you answer the question with a "no," you immediately rule out forgiveness. So, even if you are leaning toward no, you need to overrule yourself and go with yes.

- Can I be self-compassionate?

  - The hope is that you can be self-compassionate, and the reality is that you can. Perhaps not immediately, but self-compassion can be learned, and you have to be willing to learn how to be self-compassionate.

- What good can I do to feel better emotionally?

  - You could get involved in a charity or outreach program that garners positivity. When you have a source of positivity, your mental well-being improves, and when you find a better emotional state, letting go doesn't seem like such an arduous task.

- How can I facilitate personal growth?

  - Yes, your answer should be "by letting go." Even if you are not ready to do so, the realization brings you closer to the point of forgiveness.

Chapter Summary

An inward look in the form of introspection, accompanied by journaling, is a useful way to work toward letting go. You need to understand where your anger or resentment comes from. You can then write down all associated emotions, identify limitations, and consider the bigger picture. Mindfulness is a practice that can direct your focus to the present and allow you to really experience the mundane parts of life more deeply. Forgiveness meditation is a follow-on from mindfulness, which works on breathing and visualization for the purposes of arriving at a point where you can let go.

Other exercises include expressive theory in the form of art, dance, music, and writing. We can't forget physical activity as a dopamine production endeavor, and to that end, you can supplement your work with gratitude runs/jogs. Finally, you have the set of seven questions, which also make up means to progress in the direction of letting go. I know that you know that it's not easy and that there will be setbacks, so let's jump to address that subject in the chapter that follows.

Chapter 5:

Navigating Setbacks

A woman by the name of Pascale Kavanagh was abused by her mother as a child. Pascale struggled to find the ability to forgive for most of her adult life, and although she suffered many setbacks, she kept going and didn't lose faith in the process. It wasn't as if Pascale wasn't prepared to forgive, but for many years, while undergoing therapy, she just couldn't cross the letting-go line. She credits therapy as a means to improving her state of mind, but it was only when her mother fell ill that Pascale found a means to forgive. Her mother had several strokes in 2010 and was confined to a hospital bed. The gravity of the situation made Pascale realize that forgiveness was possible, and she managed to muster the strength to absolutely and completely let go of her emotional pain. Pascale would spend hours reading to her mother, and when she passed away, there was a sense of calm, as Pascale saw her mother pass away, leaving her pain behind.

As you can see from Pascale's journey, forgiveness and letting go don't just happen overnight, and I want you to remember that when setbacks arise in your own personal journey.

Why Do Memories Resurface?

Sometimes, memories will be absent, and just when we think they are gone completely, something happens that brings those memories to the forefront of our minds. These occasions manifest as setbacks, and we need to understand this phenomenon. A very common occurrence that invokes traumatic memories is when someone becomes a parent. If you suffered abuse as a child, the birth of your own child can be an emotional setback. Not because you don't love your child but because of the realization that you have so much love for your child that you can't contemplate abuse at the hands of a parent.

There is a school of thought that differentiates between repressed memories and suppressed memories. The former refers to your memories being stored in your subconscious mind so that you don't consciously attach emotions or feelings to the memories, but they are still present. The latter refers to a conscious decision to avoid the memories, which can bring results. Both repressed and suppressed memories can resurface, and often, they do so at inopportune times.

Our brains aim to keep us safe, and one of the ways they do this is by storing the memories for possible future use. That is why you may not remember what you did last weekend, but you do remember what happened 20 years ago, often in sharp detail. Neurologically, our brains are unable to differentiate between a threat that we encountered 20 years ago and a threat that we face in the present. In the case of abuse, even though the abuse is over, the memory is retained as a defense mechanism that allows you to recognize a similar threat and act accordingly.

Positive Reinforcement

This is something that happens naturally in certain cases. For instance, if you work hard on a presentation in a workplace environment, and your success results in a promotion, your quality of work and commitment have been reinforced by the promotion. You can replicate positive reinforcement when you achieve small things each day. Suppose your house has been in need of cleaning, and you go ahead and give it a good spring clean; you can reward yourself with praise by saying "well done" or "good job" to yourself. Doing this is not going to make you forgive or allow you to predict the resurfacing of a memory, but it is the positivity that it creates that improves your mental well-being and gives you the tools to deal with resurfaced memories in a positive way.

Dealing With Painful Memories

Dwelling on negativity in any form is not good for your mental health, but because painful memories pop up when you aren't expecting them, they can surprise you unpleasantly. If you have the tools to deal with them when they pop up, you can reduce their negative impact on you and eventually break the cycle of negativity.

You need to pay attention to your thinking patterns, not only when the memory surfaces but prior to the experience. This allows you to develop a clearer perspective and anticipate how you will deal with those memories when they arrive. It is also necessary to consider how you think after dealing with the memory. Part of this process is looking for solutions, one of which may be mindfulness. Other options include meditation or journaling. A tactic that can work well is setting aside time each day to sit, think, worry, and address the possibility of painful memories. I would recommend 30 minutes, worked into your everyday schedule. By doing this, you can train your brain to dismiss painful memories and other negativity when they arise outside of your allocated thinking period. We are creatures of habit, and our brains like routines, so after a bit of time, your brain will get used to your schedule, including your 30-minute daily thinking allocation.

Another method is to distract yourself, and a good way to do this is by having a few "stop signs" that you can picture using your mind's eye. The idea is that when a painful memory pops up, you visualize your stop sign, which tells your brain to stop focusing on the memory. You can create a vision of an actual stop sign, but anything else that you find easy to visualize can work. Personally, I use three things: a red triangle, an ocean wave, and the shade of a tree. These work for me, and you may want to try them out; alternatively, find something else that works for you.

Cognitive Restructuring

Also called cognitive reframing, this technique allows you to identify negative or harmful thoughts and replace them with positive and useful thoughts. Like most other skills, it is difficult at first but becomes easier the more you practice. We all experience cognitive distortions, which are inaccurate thought patterns, and they can be restructured. Even if our thinking is cognitively correct, we can still restructure it to create better outcomes. In any event, resentment can be a result of distorted cognition regarding the feelings and emotions that make up resentment as a whole.

Awareness

You know by now that you have to be aware of something if you want to change it. When someone betrays your trust, you may experience the usual emotions, like anger, frustration, and even hate, which combine to fuel your resentment. The first step is acknowledging those feelings and emotions when they arise, but also when undertaking exercises such as journaling. You may start to notice patterns, such as feeling anxious before meeting friends, because one of the people who will be there once publicly embarrassed you. This is good progress because it allows you to notice the association consciously.

Questioning

Using the example of public embarrassment, you need to question whether or not you are justified in feeling anxious. The answer may be yes, and if it is, you should realize that the other person has a hold over you that you are *allowing* them to have. You either need to change that answer to no, or if it is no, you need to figure out what needs to happen for you to stop feeling anxious in the situation. The answer is, of course, letting go of resentment and forgiving the person who hurt you emotionally.

Restructuring

You can again call on journaling to assist in restructuring your thought pattern, among the other techniques that you have learned. Alternatively, you can create phrases that remind yourself that the past or the specific event that happened in the past will not control you. If you keep telling yourself that you are moving forward and taking control of your emotions, then those words will become actions, and positive ones, of course.

Guided Imagery

This is an offshoot of cognitive restructuring and is gaining momentum with therapists, especially in the sphere of helping patients deal with memories and associations that appear unexpectedly. It works on a stage-by-stage basis and calls on visualization. Because it is guided, the process is best practiced with a therapist, but like meditations, you can find guided imagery sessions on most music-sharing platforms, as well as YouTube.

Life Event Visualization

This could be an event of multiple events that took place years ago or something fairly recent. Perhaps you went through a difficult breakup because your partner was unfaithful or missed out on a promotion at work, which was given to someone with less experience than you. In the latter situation, there could be resentment toward your co-worker and your boss. You will be asked to close your eyes and call up images of what happened on the day that you found out you were cheated on or the meeting with your boss in which you were told that your colleague would be promoted. Try to have as clear a vision as possible, and you will more than likely experience the feelings and emotions that were present at the time of the incident.

Reinstatement of a Specific Image

This is an extension of the above visualization, but instead of focusing on the experience as a whole, your therapist will ask you to choose an image and pay close internal attention to it. When I say an image, I mean an object associated with the incident. Perhaps it is the chair that your ex-partner was sitting in when you confronted them after having found out about the infidelity or in the work situation; it could be an image of your workstation at the moment you sat down after receiving the bad news.

Feeling Focusing

The focus in this step is not on how you felt at the time but how you feel at the present moment. With your eyes still closed, your therapist will ask you to attach a sensory experience to the feeling or feelings. You may notice that you are shaking, your palms are sweating or your heart is beating faster. From this point, your therapist will begin assessing the image and feelings to establish their deeper meaning.

Prompted Soliloquy

A soliloquy involves speaking what you are thinking or feeling and considering your mental image of the object; you will be prompted to speak from the position of the object. This part is quite abstract, and it doesn't suit everyone, but if you try it, have an open mind. You might describe the chair eating your partner up or your workstation exploding.

Summarizing and Reframing

Your therapist will ask you to open your eyes, and they will provide a detailed summary of what they have learned about you and your associations with the past event. If there are inaccuracies, you will be requested to correct them before being guided through ways of reframing your feelings and emotions. Instead of harboring hurt, you will reframe the situation as a relief that your partner cheated on you because it resulted in a breakup and, furthermore, that you are better off. In respect of the promotion situation, you will be guided in the direction of accepting that you were unfairly treated and encouraged to explore other career opportunities.

The whole idea is to approach your past situations differently and to view them as positive events or blessings in disguise. When you truly accept that these situations were positive, or at the very least revealed something positive or gave you a push to make a change, the events will become less significant and, hence, no longer setbacks.

Positive Self-Talk and Affirmations

If you were told as a child that you were not good enough, would never be successful, and had no prospects in life, the chances are that you believe those things, especially if you heard them regularly. Chances are that the result is negative self-talk, which limits personal growth and forms another barrier against forgiveness. There are four major ways in which negative self-talk transpires.

Personalizing

You blame yourself for everything. Suppose you were invited out to dinner with friends, but it was canceled at the last minute. You start thinking that the cancellation was because your friends didn't want to spend time with you. However, the actual reason is that one of the attendees had to rush to see his mother, who had fallen ill.

Magnifying

You focus on the negatives only and filter out the positives. For instance, you received five compliments about the quality of your work and one criticism. By ignoring the five compliments and dwelling only on the criticism, you magnify the negative and filter out the positive.

Catastrophizing

You expect the worst in every situation without opening yourself up to the possibility that things could go well instead of going badly.

Polarizing

You only see good or bad and nothing in between while neglecting to understand that there can be good and bad in many situations.

Below I will set out some examples of negative self-talk and affirmations, and how you can turn them into positives.

Negative	Positive
I will never be able to do that. It's too hard.	It may be hard, but I will give it my best shot.
There is no way that this will work.	I will play around with options and make this work.
I am boring and nobody finds me interesting.	I have family and friends that love me for my personality.
Nothing good will ever come of this situation.	This situation has the potential to uncover great things.
I will never succeed	I will keep trying until I succeed.

To take the affirmation side further, you can write down various different affirmations on pieces of paper. Keep one in your sock drawer, one next to your toothbrush, one on the fridge, etc. Every time you grab a pair of socks, brush your teeth, or open the fridge, you can read out the affirmations. Even if you don't pay full attention to them, just saying them is helpful in retraining your brain to err on the side of positivity.

Positive self-talk and affirmations can be useful when you face setbacks or come across situations that evoke adverse feelings and emotions.

Tools and Techniques for Resilience

Life is an emotional rollercoaster, no matter who you are, and we all need to show resilience from time to time. When unplanned emotional situations crop up, often in the form of setbacks, our resilience can be tested, which is why we should all work on developing resilience on a regular basis.

- purpose

    o Finding a sense of purpose can help with resilience, whether it is fulfillment from a job, a hobby, a relationship, or charity work, to give a few examples.

- believe in your abilities

    o This is why you should pursue a career involving something that you enjoy and are good at. Self-belief is a powerful tool in emotional management.

- a strong social network

    o By having people who care for you and want the best for you, you have a network that can help and support you during tough times.

- be open to change

    o Change happens, sometimes slowly, and other times fast. Having a mentality that you will embrace change makes you more versatile and, thus, resilient in the face of unexpected situations.

The more experience that you gain in life, the better you come at displaying resilience, and it is a virtue that can serve you well when it comes to dealing with setbacks.

Self-Love for Forgiveness

We have not yet spoken much about forgiving ourselves for mistakes that we have made or acts that we regret, which affect only us. But in order to practice self-forgiveness, you have to have love for yourself. This is easier said than done because it is often the case that we beat ourselves up about things instead of practicing self-forgiveness. Let's say that you had a troubled relationship with your sister, and you kept telling yourself you would patch things up, but she passed away before you took action. Firstly, you need to understand your emotions, one of which may be guilt. Then, it is about accepting the situation as is. There is nothing you can do to go back and patch things up, and accepting that fact is important. During the acceptance process, you need to be kind to yourself, dispense with judgment, and resolve to learn from your mistakes. It isn't easy, but when you let go, your guilt will be eased, and your love for yourself will become renewed.

Chapter Summary

Memories have a way of resurfacing without warning, especially if they relate to past emotional pain. Positive reinforcement and congratulating yourself for small achievements can assist with your state of mind and allow you to deal with painful memories more effectively. Through awareness, questioning, and restructuring, you can adjust your cognition to the extent that you no longer allow the past to control you. Guided imagery, as well as self-talk and positive affirmations (sock drawer, toothbrush, fridge), are good ways to turn around tendencies to engage in negative self-talk. You can build resilience by finding purpose, believing in yourself, creating a strong social network, and embracing change. When it comes to self-forgiveness, you need to cultivate self-love by understanding your emotions, accepting what you can't change, and being kind to yourself without judgment.

Forgiveness is the key to creating a better and brighter tomorrow, and I am going to tell you all about these concepts in the next chapter.

Chapter 6

Building a Future on

Forgiveness

What if you could envision a future that is not burdened by the past? What would that future look like? I will let you answer those questions because you know what you would like your personal future to look like. But most importantly, I want you to believe that a future void of past emotional pain as a factor that holds you back is *definitely* possible.

The Importance of Self-Preservation

In a way, most of our lives are about self-preservation. We look left and right before we cross the street; we don't pick up snakes or touch hot stove plates. Well, I guess some of us do, but the point is that we go through life trying to prevent ourselves from getting hurt so that we can preserve our lives. This also applies to the mental well-being side of things; looking after your mental well-being is a very important part of self-preservation. There are measures that you can put in place to preserve your mental health, which contributes to further self-preservation as time passes, i.e., into the future.

Get to Know Yourself

You obviously know yourself, but do you *really* know yourself? Perhaps you struggle with your job because it is a high-pressure environment, and you are not cut out for working under extreme pressure. This scenario is quite common, but we get so wrapped up in our lives that we don't stop to consider what we actually want and what we are actually like as people. You could be an introvert without even realizing it, but a clear sign is if you feel emotionally exhausted after social events. You can figure yourself out to an extent by asking these types of questions. Maybe you want to expand your skill set and to do so; you can have a go at some new hobbies or look for interests that you may not have looked for previously. By doing these things, you can get to know yourself more fully, and in doing so, you also get to know the best way to treat yourself for the best chance of effective self-preservation.

Set Boundaries

People get taken advantage of because they either don't set boundaries or fail to enforce them. For many individuals, saying "no" can be difficult, and avoiding saying it can lead to self-sabotage. If you say "yes" to keep others happy, you are only doing yourself a disservice. You need to be clear on what your boundaries are and firm when it comes to enforcing them.

Make Time for Relaxation

Whether it is a yoga session, half an hour of reading, a slow walk, listening to music, lying on the beach, or any other activity, you need rest and recovery time. Otherwise, the stress of life can get in the way and negatively impact your mental well-being. As you know, mindfulness exercises and meditation are really good ways to bring relaxation into your life. Many of us take for granted how vital it is to preserve our mental health.

Exercise and a Balanced Diet

Getting takeout and grabbing a chocolate bar from the cupboard is so easy after you finish dinner. It is also very easy to lie on the couch, scroll through Instagram, or watch Netflix instead of exercising. But remember, healthy eating and exercise are both great for body and mind. If you struggle in either regard, you could take a cooking class, which will be fun, relaxing, and good preparation for a healthy meal. On the exercise front, all you need is 30 minutes per day, four days a week. I am not saying that you can't eat an unhealthy meal here and there or that you must never use social media or watch Netflix, but the secret is...balance.

Be Prepared for Change

We did discuss this under the resilience section in the previous chapter. Keep in mind that adapting to change is necessary for self-preservation. If your job requirements change, you have to embrace that change so you perform at work. Your emotional circumstances might change, and you have to change with them.

More About Boundaries

Setting boundaries is important, as discussed, and sticking to them is important, also as discussed. It is time to go deeper into the concept of boundary setting in different situations so that you are absolutely clear on the specifics and why they are necessary to protect yourself and others. Depending on you as a person, you may have strict boundaries or open boundaries. The former would keep other people at a distance, limit close relationships, and perhaps create a sense of detachment with romantic partners. If your boundaries are more relaxed, you might find it difficult to say "no," have a tendency to overshare and have a fear of rejection. Ideally, you want to be somewhere in the middle, but obviously, I can't dictate *your* boundaries; that is up to you. We can divide boundaries into five categories.

Physical

Some people are huggers, others prefer a handshake, some may be comfortable with a high five, and others prefer a simple "hello" without any physical contact. You need to establish your physical boundaries in a friendship, work situation, or any type of relationship. You may not have thought of it, but if someone is constantly patting you on the back or giving you a friendly (what they perceive to be friendly) punch on the shoulder, it is very possible that you will become uncomfortable and start to develop negative feelings toward that person. It can be tough to set these types of boundaries if you are a people pleaser, but remember, it is for your own good!

Sexual

Any form of sexual abuse is an absolute travesty, and if you were the victim of such behavior as a child, your boundaries were very much crossed. At a young age, those boundaries exist automatically, and in the case of abuse, your intimate relationships as an adult are likely to be affected. Whether you were or were not sexually abused, you need to be absolutely clear on your sexual boundaries when you begin a romantic relationship.

Intellectual

This doesn't necessarily mean your intelligence but rather your boundaries regarding thoughts, opinions, and views. It is impolite and can also be offensive when someone pushes their views onto you or when they dismiss your views. We should be able to have conversations, offer different opinions, and respect each other at the same time.

Emotional

Going back to the strict versus open boundaries, in an emotional context, some people are more comfortable sharing their feelings, and others prefer to hold their feelings close to them and only talk about those feelings to certain people. As a matter of interest, entering therapy is difficult from an emotional perspective. While a therapist has a duty to respect your boundaries, in a therapy situation, you will have to be partial to opening up your boundaries for the purposes of emotional healing.

Financial

There is a lot of pressure, sometimes self-imposed, when it comes to finances because of the desire to appear wealthy. However, you should not be financing expensive vacations on a credit card or taking out loans to live a lifestyle that you think will impress others. I am not here to lecture you on how to spend your money, but you need to be clear on your financial boundaries.

How to Set Them

You do have boundaries, even though you don't think about them. If you don't like being hugged, that is a boundary, but there is a chance that you haven't given the actual boundary a great deal of thought. It is a good idea to sit down with pen and paper and write down your boundaries, which will provoke thought into the concept, and I would like to give you some tips on how to do so.

- Think about the reasons for setting boundaries and the reasons behind your *personal* boundaries.

- Resolve to set boundaries early on in any type of relationship. If the other person doesn't know what your boundaries are, then the chance of crossing them is much higher.

- Be consistent with your boundaries.

- Make sure you are not scared to let others know what your boundaries are. They are personal, and nobody has the right to judge them or cross them.

- If and when your boundaries are crossed, you need to communicate that to the person or people who have crossed them.

If you expect others to respect your boundaries, then you also have the duty to respect theirs.

Choosing Healthy Relationships

Forgiveness can be somewhat of a double-edged sword when it comes to healthy relationships. On the one hand, if you are close to someone, it may be easier to forgive, but on the other hand, if someone who you are close to hurts you emotionally, it can be more difficult to handle the hurt because of the closeness of the relationship. Boundaries also come into play quite strongly because in a close relationship, there should be enough respect to prevent the other person from crossing your boundaries. However, there are no two ways about it when I say that healthy relationships should always be the aim.

I am not just talking about romantic relationships, but all types. You want to have a healthy relationship with your boss and with your colleagues at work, but if you are being taken advantage of and having your boundaries crossed, those are not signs of a healthy relationship. The point is that you should choose people in life who are unlikely to cross your boundaries but have the resolve to address any issues that arise, with the potential of creating resentment. That brings me to communication, which is one of the hallmarks of a healthy relationship.

How to Build Strength and Trust

If there is a lack of trust, chances are that the relationship is not a healthy one. When you build trust, you also strengthen your relationship, and there are several things you can do in order to establish trust and maintain it, resulting in a strong relationship.

- keep your word

    o If you make promises and don't follow through, the other person or people involved will start to lose trust in you. In the same breath, never make promises that you know you can't keep.

- effective communication

    o You may think that you are communicating well in a relationship, but in order to be sure, you need to ascertain whether the other person is understanding your efforts to communicate. Miscommunication has been the cause of many disputes in a plethora of situations, which is what you want to avoid.

- small steps

    o You need to prove your trustworthiness, and at the same time, you need to get proof of trust. It flows both ways. So, don't be too eager to trust, and be cautious of the other person's trust in you.

- be careful when making decisions

- Some of us are "heart on sleeve" types but always try to take your time when making decisions that could impact a relationship emotionally.

- open conversation

  - Hiding things or parts of yourself during conversations will not do any favors for the health of your relationship. Absolute honesty is key, and along with it comes strength and trust.

- don't be afraid to show your feelings and emotions

  - This is harder for some, but by suppressing feelings and emotions, you are being too vague.

- admit your mistakes

  - You know about this one and how important it is!

Respect is also a large part of a strong and trusting relationship. It is something mutual that needs to be shown by both parties in order for the relationship to grow even stronger.

Relationship Red Flags

Most people have been in a toxic friendship or relationship or worked in a toxic environment, but it can take time to come to that realization. Toxicity is most definitely a breeding ground for resentment, so you should be aware of the red flags that indicate that you may be in a toxic environment, situation, or scenario.

If you feel emotionally drained after spending time with someone, either socially or one-on-one, the relationship probably has toxic traits. In addition, if a friend or partner seems to constantly put you down, even if the tone is sarcastic, jealousy could be at work or insecurity on behalf of the other person. I am not saying that you should isolate the other person immediately, but it may be the time for an open discussion, in which you talk about how they make you feel. It is, however, your choice, and easing out of that friendship or relationship may be your best option; it is a personal decision.

When it comes to family, it could become more complicated because you can't choose your family. However, you can choose, to a certain degree, how much time you spend with a family member who is not serving you the way that they should. Work situations can also get more complicated from the perspective that your choice when it comes to superiors and colleagues is quite limited. The bottom line is communication, and if that doesn't work, your next option is to look for another job.

I wish I could tell you that it is an easy fix, but what I can tell you is that the people you value in your life and who value you will always want the best for you. They are there for you, and you should be there for them regarding feelings, emotions, and difficult situations. Deep down, you will know when you are in a relationship, whatever the nature, which is toxic or on its way to toxicity.

An Amazing Story of Forgiveness

You probably remember the Columbine shooting, which made headlines across the world. If not, it happened in 1999, when two teenagers, Eric Harris and Dylan Klebold, walked into their school, Columbine High, opened fire, and killed 11 students and one teacher before committing suicide themselves. Coni Sanders, the daughter of the deceased teacher, developed a strong hatred toward Sue Klebold, Dylan's mother, and harbored anger for many years after the incident. If we look at the situation from an outsider's perspective, perhaps we would not place blame on the parents of the shooters, but it is understandable that Coni would do so.

Over time, Coni realized that she couldn't blame Sue Klebold for Dylan's actions, but this realization was not before Sue contacted Coni via email, saying that she would be willing to meet with Coni if Coni so wished. The daughter of the slain teacher was angry. Although she agreed to the meeting, Coni's words at the time were: "I wanted Sue to be awful, I wanted her to be terrible, I wanted it to be this, 'Yup I knew it she's a terrible person. She raised a terrible kid, and that kid killed my dad'" (Hallowell, 2019).

When the two women met, Coni realized that she had not gotten what she wanted and that perhaps she didn't *actually* want Sue to be a horrible person. They sat together for over two hours, and afterward, Coni described Sue as peaceful, compassionate, and comforting. She went on to say, "I could be the best parent in the world, and my kids might still make choices and decisions that I don't agree with" (Hallowell, 2019).

Coni's anger and resentment dissipated quickly, and she felt that although she was unequivocally forgiving, there wasn't anything to forgive. She was able to let go of the emotional pain that had consumed her for nearly 20 years prior to meeting Sue, and as of the time of writing, the two are great friends who meet regularly and find comfort and solace in each other.

There is so much that we can take from this story, and when you are struggling to let go, I want you to think back to what you have just read and take inspiration to aid your pursuit of being able to forgive.

Chapter Summary

Life is about self-preservation, and to practice it, you need to get to know the real you, make time for yourself, and do your best to maintain a healthy lifestyle. Basically, you are responsible for looking after yourself. Boundary setting is part of self-preservation from a physical, sexual, intellectual, and financial standpoint. It is incumbent on you to choose healthy relationships by building strength and trust. To do so, you need to keep your word, communicate effectively, be cautious, and have open and honest conversations. You know how to identify relationship red flags, and you have the wonderful story of Coni Sanders and Sue Klebold to call on for inspiration to forgive. So, let's take a leap forward into the next chapter, in which we will discuss how to reach your hand out...you'll see what I mean.

Chapter 7:

Extending the Olive Branch

Things are not always what they seem, and I would like to open this chapter with a story about how years of anger and resentment could have been prevented. It does have a happy ending, but I want you to use it as motivation to repair emotional wounds as soon as you can rather than letting them fester. The names have been changed to protect the identity of the people involved.

The situation could be described as a family feud. Mary and Peter married just after World War II and had four children: Craig, Brenda, Megan, and Gail. They didn't have the best childhood, as Peter drank heavily. He was verbally abusive but never got physical with Mary or any of the children. Peter died of a heart attack when all four children were in their 20s, but only Craig, Brenda, and Megan attended their father's funeral. From the day of Peter's death, Gail cut off the rest of the family. When she got married, none of the family were invited, and despite numerous attempts to contact Mary and her siblings, Gail refused to entertain their efforts. The strange thing was that nobody knew the reason for being completely isolated. Craig made the biggest effort to get Gail to open up and explain what was going on, but to no avail. Gail and her husband, David, had children of their own who never got to meet their uncle, aunts, and grandmother.

Almost 20 years after Peter passed away, Mary lost her battle with breast cancer. Gail and David very unexpectedly attended the funeral but stood at the back of the church without acknowledging anyone at all. Craig gave a speech, during which he noticed Gail and David. He was taken aback, but somewhere in his mind, he felt that their attendance was some form of reaching out. After the proceedings had finished, Craig anticipated that Gail and David would leave immediately, so he walked out of a side door and headed for the church gates. His plan was to stop Gail and David's car if they did indeed try to leave. Craig didn't know what he would do or say, but he got to the gate before the car. He broke down in tears while standing in the road, and for some reason, the sight of her brother's visceral pain made Gail ask David to stop the car. She jumped out and embraced Craig, and soon enough, Brenda and Megan had arrived to join the embrace. Everyone was crying, and as it carried on, it was as if all the emotional pain was flowing out of the four siblings. No words were spoken for 10 minutes, and it was as if some invisible healing force had taken over.

When everyone had calmed down, a decision was made to go back to Craig's house and just *be* siblings again. Craig's wife, along with Brenda and Megan's husbands, took the various children to lunch so that Craig, Brenda, Megan, and Gail could be alone with each other. The four of them began to discuss their childhood, and the reminiscing that occurred made it seem like they had never been apart. After quite some time, Gail said that she was ready to talk about why she had cut the whole family off. Gail had always wanted to go to university, but Peter, who was a monogynist and believed that women should not become college students, had forbidden her to do so. When she was 18, Gail applied for a scholarship to a university but never heard back. She would have had no other way to pay for her studies, so she joined the workforce as a secretary. Shortly after Peter had died, Gail started going through his belongings, photographs, and files, where she discovered a letter from the university informing her that her application for a scholarship had been successful.

Gail took her anger from that day and turned her back on the entire family, under the assumption that, at the very least, her mother had been aware of the situation. The dour siblings sat and talked about absolutely everything until the early hours of the morning, and Gail was astounded at how her anger dissipated, along with any resentment that she held for the father. There was no reason for Gail's brother and two sisters to hold anything against her, and a decision was taken to put the past 20-odd years behind them and move forward as a family...and just like that, in what seemed an instant, forgiveness filled the room.

There is a lot that can be unpacked in the above story. Still, the most important point is that had Gail raised her grievance with the family all those years ago, forgiveness could have been forthcoming, and she wouldn't have spent such a large portion of her adult holding onto emotional pain. What I want you to take from Gail's experience is that starting the forgiveness ball rolling as soon as possible is better for everyone involved, especially the person who is willing to forgive.

Genuine Remorse Versus Empty Words

An empty apology is easy to spot, and if you are giving an apology, you need to be absolutely genuine and express your remorse. Your first port of call is achieving that level of remorse, which is often not difficult. Remorse, however, can be unpleasant to deal with, which is why a heartfelt apology and a request for forgiveness, if granted, will ease the feelings of remorse. What follows are some tips on making your apology sincere and meaningful. A word of warning: Don't try to "act" out a heartfelt apology if you have not yet reached the point where you are ready to apologize.

Your Means of Communication

The easier path is to apologize via text, but I always advise apologies to be done in person. But if that is not possible, the second best option is over the phone. Texting really is too easy and very inauthentic. In other words, a hollow apology is more often sent via text.

Take Full Responsibility

An apology should not start off with a "Sorry, but..." There are no buts, certainly not in the early stages. But after a conversation ensues, the other party, if your apology is clearly remorseful, will probably admit to mistakes or wrongdoing on their part.

Be Specific

You know what you did wrong, and it is your responsibility to admit to it instead of trying to skirt around the issue. Again, this is a sign of a genuine apology with honest intentions.

Use Body Language

Don't focus too much on your body language, as you could come across as if you are trying too hard. But don't laugh or be overly engaged, either. Use body language that shows you really care and that you are taking the apology seriously.

Listen and Validate

While an apology is taking place, the other person may tell you about their anger, how you made them feel, and any ill wishes that they have toward you. Don't interrupt; take the person's words to heart, and validate them by telling the other person that you understand and that they are completely justified to feel the way they do.

Making Amends

If it is something that you can correct, offer to do so, and if you can't, then offer to do something nice for the other person as a way of making amends.

Accept the Outcome

The other person might say that they are not prepared to forgive you, and even though that's not what you want to hear, you are unlikely to change their mind at that moment. Some people need to let the apology sink in and take some time before they accept. Don't be too concerned if you are not forgiven there and then, but entertain the possibility that you may be forgiven later.

Pride and Ego

If you are too proud to apologize, or your ego is preventing you from apologizing, then you are not coming from a genuine place. You are the one who put yourself in this position, so putting your pride on the shelf, pushing your ego aside, and being heartfelt is the least you can do.

Active Listening

If you are the giver *or* receiver of the apology, there will probably be some discussion. Respect is still important, and you both need to allow the other person to speak without interrupting or just dismissing everything that they say. Active listening shows that you are truly invested and that the apology and conversation are important to you.

When someone is talking, you should be interested, and one way to maintain and display your interest is by asking relevant questions and using certain statements. For example:

When someone is talking, you should be interested, and one way to maintain and also display your interest is by asking relevant questions and using certain statements. For example:

- If I understand you correctly, you are saying X, Y, and Z, right?

- o If you don't understand fully, the other person then has the opportunity to clear up what you may not have understood.

- Could you please tell me more about that?

  - o If you are asking for more information, it shows that you have good intentions when it comes to being prepared to hear things that you might not like hearing.

- Is there anything you think that you could have done differently?

  - o This can be quite a sensitive question, so get your timing right.

- I'm sorry to interrupt, but I'm not sure I'm following. Please can you explain it to me again?

  - o Once more, it shows investment in the conversation and being absolutely clear on an occasion that can be an emotional one.

  - o And yes, I did say interrupting is bad, but if it is to clarify something, you are well within your rights to interrupt.

Empathy

You already know what empathy is, and to that end, I am going to tell a true story of a man who put himself in a position to understand someone else who is in the same position. In 1959, a white man from Texas named John Howard Griffin moved to the segregated and racially charged deep South. He used sun lamps and medication to darken his pigment and spent time working in Mississippi, Georgia, and South Carolina over a six-week period.

Griffin was a regular victim of racial abuse, both verbal and physical. He learned how demeaning it was to have to walk miles just to be able to use a toilet and experienced what it was like to have white people take no interest in you. He learned this when he worked as a shoe shiner in New Orleans, when his customers (all white) hardly even looked at him, let alone said "please" and "thanks." Griffin went on to work as an activist alongside Martin Luther King" in the fight against segregation. Clearly, Griffin found out exactly what empathy was because he was in the exact same situation as the "other" black people.

Accepting an Apology

This is what you want to work toward. Accepting an apology is your ticket to letting go of emotional pain. Yes, I know it's difficult, but looking at the mechanics of accepting an apology may change your mind about apologies you may not have accepted in the past. You need to make it clear that you accept the apology but do it in a bold way that affirms better results in situations that may follow. Just respond with "okay" when the other person is making a big effort to extend the apology. As we looked at above, active listening is a much better, more sincere approach. Let's look at some examples.

1. I appreciate your apology, and I understand that it takes bravery. I would like to converse more with you before I consider accepting your apology.

2. You sincerity shows me that you are indeed remorseful, and because of that, I forgive you.

3. Now that you have apologized, I know that there were certain things that I could have done differently. Perhaps we could also discuss some of those.

4. I accept your apology, and I think we should talk about how we can do better in the future.

5. I accept. Let's go to the beach. (this is probably the best outcome...if genuine).

Reconciliation

You should remember me explaining that forgiveness does not have to involve reconciliation, and that is fine. But it can be very emotionally powerful as a means to letting go completely. Depending on your situation, therapy is specifically to help you get through the difficult discussions where honesty and openness are required. If you are serious about reconciliation, talking about every detail of whatever it is that happened has to be your top priority. It may require several therapy sessions to get everything out if it is a more serious scenario involving a lot of emotional pain. The process is more intricate and detailed than an apology after being 30 minutes late to meet a friend. If you are having a regular argument, you could get to the point where one party realizes that they are in the wrong and is ready to apologize. That is a good place to be, but I recommend taking a break, and spending an hour or so doing something else before having the reconciliation discussion. Lastly, keep having discussions for as long as you need, whether they are scheduled therapy sessions or regular conversations.

Pitfalls of Attempting to Reconcile

If you are unprepared for the reconciliation situation dependent, you are not taking it seriously enough. If you have a scheduled therapy session or set a time for a reconciliation-directed conversation, you need to be clear about what you would like to raise and your thoughts on whatever the subject is. Although the idea behind reconciliation is for everybody to be treated equally and vice versa, it is not uncommon for one, both, or several parties to try and assert power over the conversation. Seeing yourself as better than the other person or in a superior position does not lead to equal treatment. I say again that equal treatment is essential. Returning to empathy, if you can't put yourself in the other person's position, even if it is only partially, reconciliation becomes much more likely. If the discussions extend to a point where voices are being raised and condescending words exchanged, it is best to cut the reconciliation attempt short, with the intention of coming back when things have calmed down emotionally. Furthermore, reconciliation doesn't work when one person goes in with completely unrealistic expectations. You are having an emotional negotiation, and you have to be prepared to negotiate amicably. If you intend "winning" or "proving that you're right," then you aren't ready for reconciliation, and lastly, if you are not prepared to follow up, you are also not ready.

Chapter Summary

I implore you to learn from Gail's story and how she could have let go of her resentment way earlier than she ended up doing. When apologizing, you want to be remorseful and avoid using empty words. In-person is always best, followed by a conversation over the phone or, at worst, via text. Taking responsibility, being specific about the details of your apology, listening to the response, and offering to make amends are the ingredients for a genuine apology. Don't let your pride or ego get in the way! Active listening involves showing the person who you are talking to that you are invested and interested in what they have to say. Take note of John Howard Griffin's story and use it to motivate you to do what it takes to be empathetic. You will only sincerely accept an apology if you *really* want to, so please take note of the hypothetical statements made upon receiving an apology. Finally, reconciliation requires full investment, and it has to be genuine. Otherwise, the attempt won't be successful.

And onto lack of forgiveness...

Chapter 8:

Dealing with "Unforgiveness"

When you are not forgiven, you may find it difficult to let go. We will discuss this later on in the chapter, but for now, we will look at being unable to forgive oneself, starting with the difficulties involved.

Challenges to Self-Forgiveness

You may get annoyed at yourself for losing your keys, but that does not require much self-forgiveness. Alternatively, you could have caused major emotional hurt, which can be extremely hard to forgive yourself for various reasons.

- you are afraid of being selfish

  - The thing is that you have to be selfish at times. Ask yourself if it is better to forgive yourself and have peace of mind or not forgive yourself and hold onto the emotional pain. I know you know the answer, and you also know that it's more difficult than just saying it.

  - Please don't mistake this for me saying that it is okay to be selfish in every situation. Regarding how you deal with other people and strangers in your life, you should not be selfish in situations where selfishness is uncalled for.

- feeling guilty

  - If you aren't able to accept that situations requiring self-forgiveness can be selfish, then you will continue to feel guilty and regretful.

  - While these feelings are completely normal, there are ways to ease them, and we will look at those reasons shortly.

- self-doubt

  - If you start thinking that you are not worthy of self-forgiveness or that you deserve to be in emotional pain, you will find it very difficult to forgive yourself.

You have to fully forgive yourself, and depending on the severity of the misdeed, therapy could help to limit the challenges. The other thing to consider is the fact that therapists are professionals, and while you can learn to forgive and let go on your own, with the assistance of this book, seeing a therapist, even intermittently, is never a bad idea. Just one quick word of caution: be careful when you choose a therapist. The relationship that will develop will no doubt include a lot of emotional experiences, and you need to feel comfortable with the person who is assisting you.

Forgiving Yourself

Self-forgiveness isn't too different from forgiveness, but the conversations only involve one person...yourself. Just like forgiving someone else, there are certain stages to pass through, with the ultimate goal of letting go of the painful emotions. The very first thing that you need to do is acknowledge that you are resentful. That is kind of like the starting line from which you begin the self-forgiveness journey.

Write Down Your Mistakes

Get out that pen and paper again, and jot down all your mistakes. When you have done so, read them out loud and take a few moments to consider them. You may already feel some positivity because although it is hard to admit your mistakes, you know you are moving in the right direction. If that is the case, then I recommend repeating the exercise more regularly for faster progress.

The Learning Curve

When you have finished the writing down and reading out process, you may need a break because of the potential emotional gravity of the mistake-admitting part. When you are ready, go through what you can learn from each mistake you made. Dwelling in the past is not a good thing, but in this case, you first have to consider what you could have done differently before you can return to the present and address the second mistake.

The Big Conversation

Now that you have the material for the conversation, you can activate your inner voice and talk it out with yourself. Try to adopt two perspectives, that of you as resentful and without resentment. When you come to solutions, different perspectives, and how you will benefit from forgiveness, write it down. You will be able to see how the choice of non-resentful you, as opposed to resentful you, is the better way to go.

Know What You Want

Think of forgiving a friend and how it would feel from their end. That is the same way *you* want to feel, and you deserve to feel like there are no hard feelings and everything has been dealt with effectively enough to move on in a positive way.

Some people find it harder to forgive themselves than others. For example, if there is a car accident, and one driver ends up in a wheelchair, the other driver may feel at fault, even if it is out of their control. This is one of the hardest circumstances in which to forgive yourself, but you have to remember that letting go of the guilt by forgiving is the best thing for your mental well-being.

Self-Imposed Guilt

If you find yourself in a situation that calls for self-forgiveness, even if you are able to forgive, you may still have some guilt left over. The guilt is from the remorse and regret that you have, which is normal, but there are ways to ease your mind and erase the guilt.

- Keep reminding yourself that making mistakes is frighteningly normal and that you are not unique in making them.

- Be aware of your guilt, and when the thoughts start creeping in, use the stop sign technique to direct those thoughts elsewhere.

- Stand up to your harsh critic inside, and remember to treat yourself the way that you would treat a close friend.

- Talk about it with friends, family, or your therapist.

- Tell your guilt that you will use it as a learning opportunity.

What to Do When You Ask for Forgiveness, but It Is Not Given

Earlier, I stated very briefly that not everyone forgives after an apology and that forgiveness might be delayed. To take the point further, I'd like to look at the best way to handle things when forgiveness is not forthcoming.

- don't take it back

- o You should have gone in intending to accept the outcome, whether good or bad. Taking your apology back shows that you are not truly remorseful, in any case.

- o If there was a chance of future forgiveness, taking the apology back will probably destroy that chance

- don't get defensive

  - o Avoid undoing the good work you did during your apology by getting your backup if it is not accepted. Not provoking confrontation is your aim.

- give the other person space

  - o Allowing the other person time to think, consider, and re-consider is much more likely to result in forgiveness, as opposed to being in constant contact after the apology.

- let your actions speak

  - o Show that you are truly sorry for your actions, but not in a way that is overbearing or smothering.

  - o You also don't want to look like you are trying too hard, so find a balance between too much, and not enough.

- ask to revisit the issue

  - o But not immediately.

- If a decent amount of time has passed, you can consider approaching the other person to see if they would be interested in a follow-up conversation.

Basically, you have to be resilient and take it on the chin. Be patient, and chances are, there will be an acceptance in the near future. But, if it doesn't come, take solace in the fact that you have done everything from your side. Also, don't be self-judgmental or think that you don't *deserve* to be forgiven.

Should You Forgive?

The short answer is yes, but if you are the surviving spouse of someone who is murdered, the reality is that you may never be able to let go of resentment, even though the killer is in jail. That is absolutely positively understandable because the anger and resentment are so strong. If you have ever listened to an interview with a survivor or seen a survivor talk in a documentary, you will have noticed that the ones who are able to forgive are at peace, compared with the ones who cannot forgive and who suffer emotional pain on an ongoing basis.

If you are reading this book and face the situation that I have just described, I hope you have realized that with the right steps, you can even forgive a murderer and, in so doing, improve your own quality of life. As I have said before, forgiveness does not have to be accompanied by reconciliation, and you don't even necessarily have to tell the other person that you forgive them. If you know in your heart that you have genuinely forgiven the person, then you can attain a better frame of mind through genuine forgiveness. Back to the short answer: yes...if at all possible. It will benefit *you!*

Rebuilding Connections

A successful set of discussions that led to forgiveness may not have repaired the connection that was there before. Hypothetically, something was damaged, and you need to put in some time and effort to rebuild it. When trust has been broken in a romantic relationship, and forgiveness is arrived at, the emotional connection may have broken down considerably. If you are willing to forgive, you should also be willing to build your connection back up to where it was. Even in a friendship, the closeness can be negatively affected, but it is repairable after forgiveness has been given.

Everyone follows a different timeline, so you may have to wait for the other person to be ready. Essentially, you have been disconnected, and you need to slowly reconnect. If you are a couple, and one party has been unfaithful, you can start by implementing acts of service to make each other feel wanted. Altering the relationship to make it more fun by stepping out of your couple's comfort zone can be a building block on the way to regaining your emotional and romantic connection. You can see it as getting to know each other again and being sensitive to each other's wants and needs. Progress will be slow, but if you are truly remorseful and fortunate enough to be forgiven, you need to commit to the process, even if it is a slow one. If you were the offender, you have to re-earn your partner's trust, and the recommended approach is to do it very slowly. I have heard trust compared to a plate. If you drop the plate once, and it breaks, you can use super glue to fix the plate to the point where you can hardly notice that it was once broken. If you drop the plate a second time, you can never fix it properly again.

There is a difference between infidelity in a romantic relationship and a breach of trust in a friendship. Let's say you had a great idea for a Christmas party that you wanted to host and told a friend all about it, only for your friend to steal the ideas and throw the same type of party that you were planning. This is a major trust breach and may require some time apart. Easing back into the friendship in the same way as the infidelity scenario is your best approach, but it will probably happen quicker.

A breach of trust at work could have more consequences if it results in an employee being given an official warning. You, or the person involved, may be lucky to only get a warning. Still, if the result is being fired, that employer/employee connection is most probably broken without any prospects of repair. But you never know, maybe your boss or supervisor is willing to forgive, and to allow you an opportunity to prove your trustworthiness.

Building Emotional Strength

Just like the necessity to build up broken connections, you need to be able to rebuild emotional strength, which may have been weakened due to past trauma or something more recent. It takes time to recover and to reach a point of strength again, but some ways can get you there faster.

- assess where you are

    o We go through life at our own pace, and this is completely natural. However, that can mean feeling left behind. So, you should take stock of where you are in your own life and assess whether emotional strength will assist you in letting go, making a change, forgiving, or apologizing.

- have a break

  - o Let's say that you were able to forgive, and the process involved many serious discussions and honesty that hadn't completely bee there previously. Chances are that you are emotionally exhausted. Taking some time off work to recharge your batteries at home or going on a vacation can help you recover and get stronger.

- be calm

  - o Reacting too quickly, showing irritability, and being worked up are emotionally draining. Find ways to calm yourself, such as a new exercise regime, mindfulness, or meditation.

- spend time with the right people

  - o This pretty much goes without saying. The people who build you up and want you to live your best life are the ones that you should be hanging out with.

- visit your doctor

  - o You should be doing this anyway, but it is a good idea to go for a full physical examination. It may even be the case that your emotional weakness is a result of, or partially the result of, something physiological.

- try something new

  - o Give something that you have never done before a go. Use your imagination if you don't know what to do. Otherwise, you may have always wanted to try clay pigeon shooting. Now's your chance, and it could positively affect personal growth, including mental and emotional strength.

The world would be a better place if there were a rule that you have to pause for ten seconds before you react to something. That time would allow some forethought and a whole lot of arguments would be avoided. Remember to work at staying composed by exercising control over your emotions. I'm not saying that you ignore your emotions, but rather that you should be cautious to display a particular emotion outwardly. Setting goals for your emotional strength gives you something to work toward and a means to measure your improvement. You can look at the process as a challenge to take on confidently.

Emotional strength is also needed when forgiveness is not accepted. It can be very disheartening to do everything that can be done in a genuinely remorseful manner, only to be told that you are not forgiven. Sometimes, we need to move forward on our own, and the tips above should help considerably in the case of unforgiveness.

Life-Long Learning

If forgiveness is ongoing, so should learning. Not only from letting go, forgiving, and asking for forgiveness but also from a personal emotional growth angle. You should look for material that can assist you in growing and strengthening your emotions. Remember that life is one big emotional rollercoaster, and forgiveness is just a small part of the ride.

Chapter Summary

It is possible that you are struggling to forgive yourself because you feel it is selfish, or you are feeling guilty and doubting whether you deserve forgiveness. You need to overcome these things, and a good start is to write down your mistakes, read them out one by one, learn from them, and then have a tough forgiveness conversation with yourself. Guilt may be a bit slower to move away from, but to do so; you should treat yourself like a friend would and see the guilt as a learning opportunity. If forgiveness is not given immediately, it doesn't mean that it won't be given at all. Stay patient, and prove that you are remorseful. Rebuilding connections after a breach of trust in any relationship should be done gradually to earn back the trust, and if you need to build yourself up again, you can look at where you are, take a break, and spend time with the right people. All these elements of life and forgiveness gradually create changes...good ones. So, I want to move on to address the subject of transforming your life in the chapter that follows.

Chapter 9:

Sustaining a Forgiving Heart

More relationships fail than ones that succeed, which indicates a sustainability problem. There are so many reasons behind relationships that don't work out, as is the case with friendships, that sometimes run their course and come to an end without anger or animosity. In a case like that, sustenance was not possible, but not needed, either. However, forgiving and carrying on the friendship, relationship, or association requires your heart to hold and carry the forgiveness for the length of the relationship or on an indefinite basis. A garden needs rain on a regular basis to sustain growth and remain in good condition. Your forgiveness needs to be like that regular rain in every scenario in which you have expressed your forgiveness.

Daily Rituals and Practices

Anything worthwhile takes work, and you need to decide whether or not you want to work at sustaining your forgiveness. If so, which I hope is the case, you can use some of the techniques that I am about to show you on a daily basis. Don't forget that we are looking at self-forgiveness as well as forgiving others. Mindfulness and meditation are two practices that we have already spoken about, and they can be engaged in throughout the day, especially mindfulness, *because* of the focus on the "now." I am about to take you through the practices that you could apply as a daily ritual. They are not necessarily in any order, but some can be done one after the other. However, I encourage you to adapt them, change them up, and get creative (There is a little repetition from previously, but I would like to include it rather than not.)

Set Lots of Goals

You can go as far as breaking down your day and setting goals, no matter how small. When you congratulate yourself after reaching every small goal, you are flooding your brain with positivity. I am talking about tiny things, like brushing your teeth successfully, fixing a good breakfast, and completing an exercise routine. You can carry this on throughout your work day and give yourself praise for the achievements that you make at work.

Write Lists

Not in the sense of journaling but in several other contexts. Instead of going to the grocery store without a specific list of what you need, write it all down, which also means as you tick off the items you put into your account, you feel that little bit of success...positivity! Part of your lists can be affirmations, things that you are fortunate to experience, like a sunny day or the sounds of the birds chirping.

Do Everything in Order

If you have less to think about because you know your routine so well, you have more time for mindfulness. Get up at a certain time, make coffee and breakfast, shower, change, etc. Music could be part of your routine, and your favorite songs can be a real pick-me-up in the morning to get you excited about your day.

Meditation and Deep Breathing

Slowing your heart rate down and bringing calm over your body and mind are great ways to look after your mental health and generate some perspective regarding your feelings and emotions.

Be Kind

Engaging with the server or the cashier, throwing a smile or two at strangers, and helping someone out with something make you feel good. Just knowing that the other person feels good is beneficial to you, and of course, the experience is mutual.

Stretch

Even a 10-minute stretching routine has a relaxing effect and can be done in conjunction with mindfulness. Pay attention to the part of your body that you are stretching and the way your muscles feel when they are engaged and released.

Get More Social

In the world of digital nomads and working from home, it is easy to neglect the social interactions that you need. Sitting behind a screen all day and having little to no interpersonal conversations is not good for your mental well-being. We need those interactions, even if they are not of huge substance. Joking around with a colleague while you are at work counts as a positive social event.

Get Enough Sleep

Sleep is good for the body and the mind. If you only get a few hours each night, you are bound to be mentally drained. In such scenarios, it can be difficult to maintain emotional control during the day, and chances are that you will be less alert, too. To function at your optimum, you need to get seven to eight hours of good-quality sleep. Making sure your room is dark and that you don't have many distractions is a useful way to look after your sleep quality.

Exercise and Outdoor Activities

A walk on the beach or through a forest combines nature and exercise for the double-whammy of mind and body health. Doing yoga outdoors can be good for the soul, and even walking instead of driving, if you can, is healthier. Sometimes, it's good to slow everything down, including your mind!

Sit Up Straight

If you work from home, avoid sitting in bed or on the sofa while you tap away at your keyboard. Having good posture will prevent a stiff back...one less thing to worry about.

Think of Tomorrow Instead of Yesterday

If something didn't go well the day before, avoid dwelling on it. Rather, occupy your time looking forward to the next day. It will do wonders for your positivity, as well as mental and emotional management and control.

Create a Mantra

Something as simple as "be the best you can be" will work. You might want to get more elaborate or specific. Perhaps you can use a motivational line from a movie or a book that you have read. Repeat your mantra intermittently during the day, especially if you feel frustrated or negative about something.

Like Mindedness

Toxic friendships or relationships probably indicate a lack of like-mindedness, and it is always best to seek out people who are like-minded. If you share the same morals and principles and have the same or similar interests, a healthy relationship is likely to exist. Suppose you feel that a friendship or relationship is not bringing out the best in you. If you do feel this way, it might be time to look around for other like-minded individuals. Joining a sports club, even if it is at a very social level, almost guarantees at least some like-mindedness. Let's say you play softball; your new teammates have exactly the same interest in one thing, but sports lovers often tend to get on in other areas. You could join a support group or a book club, maybe a hiking club, whatever works best for you. There are many online groups and forums, such as chats about music, history, or philosophy. You may have to step outside that good old comfort zone to find people that have commonality. You will also feel a sense of community if the social connections you make support you and you do the same for them.

Finding Inner Peace

Some people spend their whole lives trapped in jobs they don't like, or relationships that are not good for their mental health, and truly finding peace illudes them. It doesn't have to be this way, though. Let's look at some tips and techniques that you can implement if you are struggling with inner peace. However, just before we get there, I would like to stipulate what a lack of inner peace could look like for the purpose of understanding what it does look like.

- being too passive, with a feeling that you are not getting as much out of life as you could

- not taking opportunities to grow as a person

- becoming reserved and quiet instead of having interesting conversations at social events

- the feeling that something bad is going to happen

- not trying something under the assumption that you will fail

So, then, what is inner peace? I am about to tell you.

- not requiring material goods or grandiose achievements to feel fulfilled

- developing a connection with yourself

- letting go of worry and anxiety

- accepting things for what they are, from your job to your social sphere, to your body, and your appearance

- being yourself no matter what other people want or expect, and being satisfied with the self that you are

- always looking for ways to better yourself

Then, there is a mindset that is a big impediment to finding inner peace, as follows:

- I will be happy if "this" or "that" happens

  - Thinking that a relationship will make things better or that getting a new job will leave you more fulfilled is the wrong attitude. These things may help, but you have to have a healthy relationship with yourself.

- hiding your vulnerabilities

  - I'm not saying shout them out from the rooftops, but being comfortable with your vulnerabilities is better for a prospective, peaceful mind.

- thinking that you should never get angry.

  - This is a common perception, but feeling your emotions, positive and negative included, is a good thing. The important thing is to exercise control over them. It's fine to be angry, but shouting, screaming, and punching are not the ways to display your anger.

- don't compare yourself to others

  - Rather, compare yourself to yourself. An example that illustrates the principal is training for a half-marathon. As you train more, your times improve, and you can compete against yourself. You are not going to measure yourself against professional runners.

- thinking you're not good enough

- o You are good enough, and nobody has the right to tell you otherwise!

- being embarrassed about your past

  - o Forgiveness, being forgiven, and moving forward, especially self-forgiveness, allows us to let go, with the benefit of not letting the past control us.

As promised, I am going to tell you about how to work toward inner peace.

- stop blaming yourself for everything

  - o Things go wrong, and that's okay. Maybe you make a mistake here or an error there, but don't castigate yourself.

- don't play the victim

  - o Constantly asking, "Why me?" is never going to make you inwardly happy. The world isn't against you, and a lot of what happens is completely random and cannot be controlled.

- avoid people pleasing

  - o You are the most important person in your life, and your well-being must come first. It might sound selfish, but it is one area that you are allowed to be selfish in.

- let go

  - o You know this all too well, and fortunately, you know how to embark on the process.

- don't be a perfectionist

  - Nobody has ever been perfect, and nobody ever will be. To expect perfection from yourself is plain unrealistic, so cut yourself some slack and carry on doing your best.

If you can learn to be satisfied on a less is more basis, you will definitely get closer to finding inner peace.

Consistency

If you want to maintain the forgiveness mentality in your brain and in your heart, you need to become consistent. Therapists are a group that aims to maintain consistency with their patients, and more often than not, it pays off in continued personal development. In day-to-day life, you need to implement consistency, especially if you are healing from trauma. Consistency also involves following through with plans. If you accept and invite or say yes to something, you should follow through with it. Remember, you don't want to be a people pleaser, so only say yes when you can do whatever it is that you are saying yes to. Another area that requires consistency is expressing yourself in a way that is appropriate for the situation. Being consistent every day and improving little by little goes a long way to looking after your mental well-being sustainably.

Chapter Summary

We should all aim to maintain a forgiving heart. One of the ways to do this is by creating daily rituals and exercises that promote forgiveness on a long-term basis but also self-growth along the way. I am talking about setting many small goals, including lists with items that can be checked off when you achieve them. Try to keep your routine the same. Incorporate deep breathing into your life, with some stretching and a bit of kindness thrown at it. You need social interactions, a good night's sleep, and an upright back! Think of tomorrow rather than yesterday, and create a mantra you repeat every day. Finding a community of like-minded people allows you to feel included and part of something positive. This is one of the tenets of inner peace. If you are struggling in this area, you may notice that you are too passive and don't take opportunities for personal growth that come your way. To develop self-connection, you need to allow your vulnerabilities to show when acceptable and in the right situation. Anger is fine as long as you have a hold on your emotions. Don't compare yourself to others or be embarrassed by your past, and make sure you are consistent in all areas of your life. Much of what we have addressed is transformation-based, and we are about to take that further in the context of large-scale change.

Chapter 10:

The Power of a Transformed Life

An act of forgiveness can change your own life and somebody else's life, even in situations where forgiveness seemed incredibly unlikely at first. Seeing that we have reached the final chapter, I would like to start off with some stories of how people's lives were transformed as a result of forgiveness and the profound impact that it had on the person forgiving and the person being forgiven. As you will see, the circumstances of all these stories were such that the people who managed to muster forgiveness must have dug deep into their hearts and souls, but with the ultimate result of growing and transforming their lives for the better.

Brandt Jean and Amber Guyger

Amber Guyger, an off-duty police officer, opened fire on an apartment and shot the occupant, Botham Jean, who sadly passed away. Guyger claimed that she thought Botha was a burglar, even though there was no evidence to suggest any form of breaking and entering. During the court case against Guyger, the State sentenced her to ten years in prison. Brandt Jean, the deceased's brother, stood up and informed everyone present that he had forgiven Amber and asked the judge whether he could hug her. The judge allowed Brandt to do so, and the two embraced for several minutes while both sobbing. Brandt's parting words were that he hoped Amber would find solace in Christianity during her time in prison. It is remarkable that Brandt was able to extend forgiveness, but he must have known that if he hadn't, the hate, anger, and resentment would have eaten him up inside.

Marietta Jaeger and David Meirhoffer

When Marietta's daughter was seven years old, a crazed serial killer, David Meirhoffer, ended the little girl's life, but his identity was not known at the time. Marietta made it her mission to find the serial killer and stated publicly that if she found him, she would strangle him to death. About a year after the murder, David Meirhoffer made a phone call to Marietta Jaeger. He was apprehended, and Marietta decided to forgive David, who later committed suicide in 1974 in his cell. Marietta contacted David's mother, and the two developed a friendship based initially on the deaths of their respective children. They would visit the graves of the kids together, and Marietta became an anti-death penalty advocate. She did a lot of work for the UN, and we can only marvel at the ability to forgive in a situation where most would not even entertain the idea.

Mark Stroman

This American man set out after 9/11 to kill anyone who may have been an Arab. He was successful in murdering two people, but Rais Bhuyian, a naturalized American citizen originally from Bangladesh, survived. Raise lost his left eye, and his face was severely disfigured. Stroman was sentenced to death, and during his time on death row, he became truly remorseful, describing himself as "an uneducated idiot" (Boese, 2021).

Remarkably, Rais decided to lead the fight against Stroman's execution, even enlisting the help of the slain men's relatives. Rais' thinking was that Stroman's death would not change anything. He wasn't successful in preventing the execution, but he did offer up full forgiveness. One has to admire Rais and his ability to forgive, even though his life and appearance were so severely altered.

Matt Swatzell and Erik Fitzgerald

Matt Swatzell was a firefighter, and after a 48-hour shift in October 2006, he fell asleep at the wheel while driving home. The result was a collision in which the driver of another var, June Fitzgerald, was killed. She was pregnant at the time and lost the baby, but her 19-month-old daughter, who was also in the vehicle, survived. June's husband, Pastor Erik Fitzgerald, was devastated, and so was Matt because he had no ill intentions whatsoever. The two men met at Erik's request and discussed the situation in great detail before Erik offered his forgiveness. Doing so was an incredible act of kindness, and Erik even testified in court, asking for a reduced sentence. The two men later became really good friends, and that fact is a testament to how amazing the human race can be.

Eva Mozes Kor

Josef Mengele was one of the most evil Nazi doctors at the Auschwitz concentration camp during World War II. He used then 10-year-old Eva as a human guinea pig before declaring her "useless" and fit only for death. Her execution was set, but a few days beforehand, Soviet Forces stormed Auschwitz, and Eva was freed. In an act of human compassion, Eva wrote a letter to Josef Mengele in which she forgave him. She called the letter a gift to him and a gift to herself. She went on to open a museum dedicated to the memory of all the other victims of Josef Mengele and became an advocate for forgiveness until her passing in 2019 at age 85.

Candice Mama and Eugene de Kock

In the Apartheid era of South Africa, where non-white citizens were persecuted, Eugene De Kock, head of a police unit dedicated to arresting and killing anti-apartheid activists, was responsible for torturing Candice Mama's father before burning him alive. De Kock was considered one of the most deplorable people in the world and went by the name "Pure Evil." He was sentenced to 212 years behind bars, and in 2014, Candice and her mother went to visit de Kock. They asked him a series of questions before forgiving him completely, and Candace attributes her act of forgiveness as one that changed her life.

Relationships Between Healing and Inspiring

It is easy to make the connections between forgiveness and healing when reading the above stories, but there is also a huge amount of inspiration that we can take from them. Just to mention one, Eva Mosez Kor mustered the ability to forgive, and there is no doubt that she harnessed her own inspiration while healing emotionally. I want you to see if you can take something away from each story in the form of motivation to forgive and inspiration to promote forgiveness and the mutual inspirational effect that it can have. By refusing to let your past trauma and experiences dictate your present and future, you are tapping into something very powerful. All of the incredible people in the true-life stories transformed their lives by forgiving when most people would hold onto hate, anger, and resentment. Be like them, and not like the "most."

Forgiveness and Community

Practicing forgiveness can strengthen a bond between two people. Sometimes, it takes work to rebuild a connection, as you know, but often, the rebuilt connection is stronger than the initial one. It might be an idea to go into your community with the idea of uniting people through the power of forgiveness. If you manage to embark on a journey like this, you will become better at forgiving yourself, and you will be able to teach others how you have been unburdened from emotional pain when you extend the olive branch of forgiveness to people who have heard you. I would like to give you some advice on how you could go about doing this, and you will see how good it could be for you, as well as others.

Raising Awareness

You can use social media to create discussions about the power of forgiveness. If you have a community hall available to you, you could invite residents in your area to listen to you talk about forgiveness, followed by group conversations. If you have really benefited from forgiveness, and there is no reason that you wouldn't, you can approach high schools in your area and offer to talk to the kids about your personal journal with resentment and let go of it. The more people who start talking about something, the more people who become aware, and a movement can grow. If you can find true passion, you could even embark on a career as a speaker and advocate for forgiveness.

Offer Help

You don't want to become a free therapist, but if you intend to involve your immediate community, then you need to be prepared to offer your help. A good way to do this is to start a support group for people who are struggling to forgive others who have been their source of emotional suffering. There is something powerful about hearing other people's stories and sharing your own. Vulnerability is a virtue that will be on display by several people in these discussion-type situations.

Bring in Experts

Whether you involve yourself in social media campaigns, talks, or group therapy sessions, there is definitely room for experts to assist you. Hosting a breakfast where a forgiveness-specific therapist gives a talk or arranging for someone who has an inspirational story to tell can be of further assistance in a community setting.

Because of technology, your community is not necessarily just your town or suburb but a wider set of people, many of whom are struggling to let go and searching for a helping hand in doing so. Just from a general mental health point of view, you may want to consider that getting involved with your community will in all likelihood, have a profoundly positive influence on your frame of mind.

Purpose Through Forgiveness

Because forgiveness is a process, it can provide you with a purpose and a notion that your existence is valuable and that you need to do all that you can to carry your purpose with you. Let's have a look at some purposes that involve forgiveness, but also other aspects of emotional well-being when it comes to yourself and others.

Purpose One: Protect Your Loved Ones

You don't want to see your loved ones suffer emotional pain, but it is inevitable at some point. By facilitating forgiveness or inspiring an apology, request for forgiveness, and a reconciliation session, you are acting in the best interests of everyone involved. You will also see a mutual understanding of self-worth and how forgiveness brings self-worth on a personal and community level.

It may also be necessary to protect your loved ones from your *own* emotional wounds. Losing your temper or snapping at someone who has done nothing wrong because of your emotional hurt is only going to make the situation worse. So, you need to know how to conduct yourself in terms of containing your emotions. The difficult thing is that we often feel so comfortable with the ones we love that we stop making an effort and slip into a situation as described above.

Purpose Two: Help People See the Errors of Their Ways

You should remember that forgiveness is not only about right and wrong, but you might feel the need to educate the other person on an error that they made. If so, do it kindly and in a way that is helpful and not condescending. At the same time, you should be prepared to accept and take responsibility when your own errors are pointed out. Either way, it could be someone who is not directly involved in whatever it is that is affecting you negatively, but often, a pair of eyes from the outside can be good at pointing out things that you may not even have realized.

Purpose Three: Helping the Other Person Grow

If you are the one requesting an apology or pointing out to someone that they have caused you emotional harm, it is a chance for personal growth on behalf of the other person. There are, of course, times when you have been hurt, although the other person has not realized it. Perhaps a fault will be revealed, and after it has been revealed, the other person will realize that they need to work at changing a part of themselves. The mutual value is found in the fact that the other person understands that they have erred, and based on that understanding, they will probably apologize and allow you to let go of any possible resentment that they were previously unaware of.

Purpose Four: Reconciliation

At the risk of repeating myself, I need to remind you that reconciliation isn't always necessary for forgiveness to be forthcoming, but aiming for reconciliation is what you should be doing. Don't push it. If the other person is not ready, perhaps they will be in the future. Give them the space that they need.

Purpose Five: Create a Culture of Forgiveness at Home

You might not be the only person in your household who is holding onto resentment and who can benefit from this book and your new knowledge on forgiveness and its incredibly positive results on the psyche. Whether you are a mom, dad, sister, brother, cousin, or friend, make it your purpose to promote forgiveness at home and among your loved ones outside of home.

Purpose Six: Improvement for Future Generations

By practicing what you preach and spreading the word about forgiveness, you could find purpose in setting examples for kids and young adults who could fall victim to ongoing resentment. We always want to see improvement through the generations, and in today's world, there are so many platforms that can be used to pass on advice through actions and education. Learning something young means that you will be better at it, and forgiveness isn't an exception to that rule.

Purpose Seven: Broadening Your Own World View

When you get into a culture of forgiveness, you start noticing things about how people treat each other. You focus more on kindness and equal treatment, plus you want to reach people with what you have learned. The realization that the world would be a better place with more forgiveness is an important one, and living that realization makes the world a better place, little by little.

The above purposes are not in a one-by-one or chronological order, and they might not all apply to you. However, I would like you to take them to heart and understand how powerful it can be to have a purpose and to achieve that purpose, whether it is one thing, ten things, or more.

Chapter Summary

Forgiveness can change your life and the lives of others through its profound power. Often, it's not easy, but you have the six motivational stories of individuals who have forgiven others in exceptionally difficult situations. By forgiving and being forgiven, there is a connection to healing and to inspiration, not only to others but to you! Involving your community in the power of forgiveness can be altruistic and uplifting, whether it is directed at online communities or your neighborhood. There is a purpose to be found in forgiveness, including protecting loved ones, helping others identify mistakes, and facilitating personal growth. Promoting reconciliation can also be seen as a purpose, but don't push it. Otherwise, you should look to assist in bettering the next generation and broadening your own worldview. And with that we come to the end of the body of this book, but don't go anywhere just yet, there is a great conclusion in summary form that is still to come. But there is a bonus chapter in store for you first.

Conclusion

Thank you for reaching this point in the book. I hope that you have enjoyed reading. I certainly had a good time writing it. My wish is that what you have just read will help you or has already started to help you think differently about hate, anger, resentment, and all the other emotions that make forgiveness difficult. You have the skills to simplify it and the techniques to go about getting that elephant off your back. I would like to leave you with a concise summary of the contents in a way that will allow you to refer to specific parts of the book if you need to go over or revisit them.

To be able to forgive, the first step is to understand forgiveness in the context of vulnerability. Forgiveness is more about you than the other person. It does not mean that the incident should be forgotten but rather retained as a learning tool. It's tough! I don't need to tell you that. We tend to hold onto pain and let emotional anchors weigh us down. Holding grudges has adverse mental health consequences, and forgiveness is your best bet, although it doesn't have to involve reconciliation.

You remember the story about the couple and the half-brothers, where forgiveness was not forthcoming, and that self-forgiveness was necessary. In situations like this, depression can set in, your mind can become occupied with negativity, and you can ruminate to the point where you have no peace. However, when forgiveness is given and accepted, responsibility is taken honestly, which is one of the components of a heartfelt apology. Spirituality could be something that you are interested in as a means to come to terms with resentment and forgiveness. It may be successful in facilitating trust and personal growth.

Before you can genuinely heal, you need to accept that you are experiencing it. Unfounded anger, among other reasons, is a sign of resentment. To get rid of your resentment, you have to be vulnerable, which makes you brave, not weak. When you are going through the healing process, you must allow yourself to feel your emotions, have clarity on them, respond instead of reacting, and be more trusting. Don't forget about the Enright and REACH models if you want to work on yourself alone or with a therapist. You can even combine these models with forgiveness letters that can be used in a support group environment if that is something that you would like to explore.

Looking inward and writing down what you find can be done in a journal. The idea is to let it all out by getting to the source of the pain, writing honestly about it, and stepping back to see the bigger picture. From there, you can let go, perhaps with the assistance of mindfulness, where you exercise deep focus. You have the example of a meditation session to use if you wish, and other options include art, dance, or music therapy. Exercise is a natural source of dopamine, and its positive effect is conducive to a more positive outlook.

Pascale Kavanagh managed to forgive her mother in later life for being abused as a child. Prior to forgiveness, painful memories can strike unexpectedly but can be dealt with through positive reinforcement, no matter how big or small. Cognitive restructuring is categorized by awareness, questioning the resentment, and restructuring. Guided imagery, which is best done with a therapist, has proven successful in the forgiveness sphere and involves visualization and focus. If you tend to personalize and magnify, you are probably prone to negative self-talk. Other signs are catastrophizing and seeing only good or only bad in different situations. It is important to switch to possible self-talk and say things like "I will keep trying until I succeed," as opposed to "I will never succeed. It's too hard." Purpose, belief in yourself, a strong social network, and a willingness to accept change are all needed to be resilient in emotionally testing situations. Don't forget to love yourself by being understanding toward yourself.

We all have to practice self-preservation, which is best practiced when you get to know yourself deeply, allow relaxation time, and lead a healthy lifestyle. Setting boundaries physically, sexually, intellectually, emotionally, and financially can help significantly...but...the golden rule...stick to them! Respecting boundaries is part of a healthy relationship, and so is keeping your word, communicating effectively, and admitting your mistakes. Another quick reminder of an inspiring forgiveness story: Coni Sanders, the daughter of the deceased teacher, and Sue Klebold, the mother whose son killed him.

While we are talking about stories, don't forget the story about Gail, whose father hid her college scholarship acceptance letter. If Gail had been open to discussion 20 years prior, she would have saved two decades of emotional pain. When apologizing, the order of methods is in-person, over the phone, or via text. The person who is apologizing must take responsibility, be specific, and not let pride or ego get in the way of a genuine apology. You can give active listening a try in an apology situation, where you ask questions, use statements to get clarity, and show that you are fully invested. If you struggle with empathy, read the John Howard Griffin/Deep South story. Reconciliation can go along with forgiveness; simply, you need to be committed, realistic, and willing to have difficult conversations.

When it comes to self-forgiveness, there are challenges that present themselves. You may feel as if you are selfish by letting yourself off and could experience guilt and self-doubt. A proven method of approaching self-forgiveness is to admit your mistakes, label them a learning curve, have a sincere conversation with yourself, and decide exactly what you want moving forward. Depending on the gravity of your resentment, a dose of guilt may remain. If you are aware of it, face up to it, and let yourself know that you don't have to be guilty in the same way that a friend would. If you ask for forgiveness but don't get it, be prepared to wait and give the other person space. If you can, you should always commit to the forgiveness process because of how beneficial it is to yourself.

In relationships that have been damaged, there is a need to rebuild the connection, which can be a slow but necessary process. You may also need to rebuild your own emotional strength. To do so, assess where you are in life and what it means to the way you feel and the emotions that you experience. Take a break if you need to, and do things to calm yourself, preferably with the right people. Get a physical examination and look for growth through a new hobby, activity, or endeavor. Life-long learning is what we should all aspire to, and you now have the tools to be a life-long learner.

Similarly to self-preservation, forgiveness should have a permanent place in your heart, and now you have the daily rituals and practices that will help you sustain forgiveness. As a reminder, you might enjoy mindfulness and meditation, but there are a number of other techniques to create positive energy throughout your day. Small goals, lists, kindness, and getting enough good sleep are a few examples, in addition to creating a stretching routine, sitting up straight, and having a mantra. Look for like-minded people to bring into your life, and aim for inner peace by not being embarrassed about the past, not entertaining self-blame, and avoiding people pleasing, along with consistency in a general sense.

Forgiveness is powerful, and the stories about Brandt Jean, Mark Stroman, and others should be motivational enough for you to take the lead. If you get the opportunity and you are interested in community well-being, you can look into giving talks, raising awareness, and offering help where you can. Doing these things is akin to finding a greater purpose through forgiveness so that you can protect your loved ones and strangers, for that matter. There is also purpose to be found, including helping others grow and promoting reconciliation. Assisting in the betterment of future generations and developing a better worldview when it comes to future prospects are also purpose-generating endeavors for you to consider.

There we have it! Now that you are much more educated on forgiveness, I would love to hear from you in the form of a rating. Please take a few moments to leave one, and let me know how much you enjoyed the book and the ways in which you are benefiting yourself by implementing what you have learned.

Bonus Chapter:

Off The Beaten Path

Nelson Mandela is possibly one of the most forgiving human beings that this world has ever seen. To put you in the picture, the former president of South Africa was subject to treatment as a second-class citizen during apartheid. The regime was all about segregation, where non-whites had to travel third class on trains, were not allowed on the same beaches as white people, had to carry a pass to be out on the streets, and were moved from their homes and placed in areas far from where the whites lived.

Mandela, a black lawyer, was in opposition to the system, and as part of the political party, the African National Congress (ANC), he orchestrated resistance to apartheid in any manner that he and his comrades were able to. Yes, there was violence involved, but when you are being ignored, sometimes violence is the way to get noticed. As a result, Mandela became a wanted man and went on the run, but was captured after the military police mobilized and tracked him down.

Mandela, along with several other non-white people who were involved in the resistance, were tried in Rivonia, Johannesburg. At the end of the hearings, and after the sentences were handed down, Mandela was staring at life behind bars directly in the face. From the confines of his prison cell, he did all that he could to communicate with the outside world. He continued to oppose apartheid and lived vicariously through his comrades who kept up the fight on the outside.

After over two decades in prison, talks regarding the end of apartheid started taking place, and after 27 years as a convict, Mandela was released. South Africa held a democratic election, and for the first time, non-whites were allowed to vote. The ANC became the ruling party, and Nelson Mandela took over the presidency. He finally had the chance to persecute the white people who had persecuted him for such a long time. However, he forgave, even though he could have taken revenge. Mandela had a vision of a united South Africa, where its citizens would live side by side, joined through equality, and that is exactly what he did.

Now, my friends, if the great Nelson Mandela could forgive and let go, considering his deplorable treatment, so can you, and I *hope* you will!

Author Biography

ABOUT THE AUTHOR

Throughout my adult life, I've had many experiences in different positions ranging from musician, to shipyard electrician, to industrial millwright electrician, to the owner of a limousine company, to the owner of a real estate investment company, to a licensed commercial instrument pilot and now to a published author.

Given my range of experiences, people kept telling me: "You should write a book, because you have a lot of good ideas." Finally, I decided to take them up on their advice. As I wrote, my stories came to life. My main purpose as an author became clear: That whoever reads my stories, they would receive more value than they expected.

So, it's my pleasure and privilege to create entertaining, educational, and informative stories for you!

R. T. Kagels

References

Ackerman, C. (2018). *Cognitive restructuring techniques for reframing thoughts.* Positive Psychology. https://positivepsychology.com/cbt-cognitive-restructuring-cognitive-distortions/#techniques-cognitive-restructuring

Aydin, D. (n.d.). *15 Quotes about light that follows darkness.* Guideposts. https://guideposts.org/inspiring-stories/stories-of-faith-and-hope/14-quotes-about-light-that-follows-darkness/

Boese, E.L. (2021). *Ten of the most inspiring stories of forgiveness that you will ever hear.* Everything Else. https://theverybesttop10.com/inspiring-stories-of-forgiveness/

Brenner, A. (2020). *5 Reasons why it's important to forgive.* Psychology Today. https://www.psychologytoday.com/us/blog/in-flux/202009/5-reasons-why-its-important-forgive

Brickel, R.E. (2017). *Why consistency is a powerful force for healing trauma.* Brickel & Associates. https://brickelandassociates.com/consistency-powerful-approach-to-treating-trauma/

Brown, L. (2023). *How to find inner peace: 10 Things you can start doing right now.* Hack Spirit. https://hackspirit.com/how-to-discover-your-inner-peace-in-4-simple-steps/

Chandra, R. (2022). *Eight questions for understanding and healing resentment.* Psychology Today. https://www.psychologytoday.com/us/blog/the-pacific-heart/202208/eight-questions-understanding-and-healing-resentment

Cherry, K. (2023). *How to forgive yourself.* Very Well Mind. https://www.verywellmind.com/how-to-forgive-yourself-4583819#:~:text=To%20forgive%20yourself%2C%20you%20should%3A%20Understand%20your%20emotions,Focus%20on%20making%20better%20choices%20in%20the%20future

Cherry, K. (2023). *Positive reinforcement and operant conditioning.* Very Well Mind. https://www.verywellmind.com/what-is-positive-reinforcement-2795412

Cherry, K. (2022). *10 Ways to build resilience.* Very Well Mind. https://www.verywellmind.com/ways-to-become-more-resilient-2795063

Cherry, K. (2021). *What is expressive arts therapy?* Very Well Mind. https://www.verywellmind.com/expressive-arts-therapy-definition-types-techniques-and-efficacy-5197564

Cherry, K. (2023). *What is negativity bias?* Very Well Mind. https://www.verywellmind.com/negative-bias-4589618#:~:text=The%20negativity%20bias%20is%20our%20tendency%20not%20only,powerfully%20than%20we%20feel%20the%20joy%20of%20praise.

Craig, H. (2019). *10 Ways to build trust in a relationship.* Positive Psychology. https://positivepsychology.com/build-trust/

Crimmins, J. (2023). *Letting go of guilt: Embracing inner peace.* https://healthnews.com/mental-health/self-care-and-therapy/letting-go-of-guilt-embracing-inner-peace/

Crimmins, J. (2023). *Master the art of accepting apologies: building a stronger relationship.* Health News. https://healthnews.com/mental-health/self-care-and-therapy/how-to-accept-an-apology/

Cuncic, A. (2020). *The connection between anger and depression.* Very Well Mind. https://www.verywellmind.com/connection-between-depression-and-anger-5085725

Cohen, S. (2020). *Understanding forgiveness.* Psychology Today. https://www.psychologytoday.com/us/blog/your-emotional-meter/202010/understanding-forgiveness

Coller, N. (2015). *Why we hold grudges and how to let them go.* Psychology Today. https://www.psychologytoday.com/us/blog/inviting-monkey-tea/201503/why-we-hold-grudges-and-how-let-them-go

Contreras, A. (2020). *Your emotional brain on resentment: Part 1.* Psych Central. https://psychcentral.com/pro/your-emotional-brain-on-resentment-part-1#1

Dedrick, C. (2021). 9 Myths about forgiveness that fool the best Christians. Crosswalk. https://www.crosswalk.com/blogs/christian-trends/9-myths-about-forgiveness-that-fool-the-best-christians.html

Everett, L. W., Toussaint, L. Griffin, B. (2018). *How to build a more forgiving community.* Greater Good Magazine. https://greatergood.berkeley.edu/article/item/how_to_build_a_more_forgiving_community

Fensterheim, S. (2019). *Surviving a relationship injury.* Good Therapy. https://www.goodtherapy.org/blog/surviving-relationship-injury-forgive-but-don%27t-forget-040820197

Fishman, S. (2023). *The anchoring effect: How it impacts your daily life.* Psych Central. https://psychcentral.com/health/the-anchoring-effect-how-it-impacts-your-everyday-life

14 Warning signs that unforgiveness is eating you alive (and what to do about it). (n.d.). Spiritual Living. https://www.spirituallivingforbusypeople.com/unforgi veness

Gillette, H. (2023). *How to be sincere in an apology.* Psych Central. https://psychcentral.com/health/how-to-make-a-sincere-apology

Gould, W.R. (2023). *13 Red flags in relationships.* Very Well Mind. https://www.verywellmind.com/10-red-flags-in-relationships-5194592

Hallowell, B. (2019). *Columbine victim's daughter reveals amazing story of forgiveness.* https://www.pureflix.com/insider/columbine-victims-daughter-reveals-amazing-story-of-forgiveness

Holland, K. (2020). *Positive self-talk: How talking to yourself is a good thing.* Healthline. https://www.healthline.com/health/positive-self-talk#_noHeaderPrefixedContent

Holler, M. (2019). *20 Daily rituals to maintain your mental health.* Mom.com. https://mom.com/momlife/daily-rituals-to-maintain-your-mental-health

Howes, R. (2023). *Forgiveness versus reconciliation.* Psychology Today. https://www.psychologytoday.com/us/blog/in-therapy/201303/forgiveness-vs-reconciliation

How to reconcile after an argument (the healthy way). (n.d.) Reconnect Counseling. https://www.reconnectcounseling.com/how-to-reconcile-after-an-argument-the-healthy-way/

Jameson-Shea, L. (n.d.). *What are some challenges or pitfalls to avoid restorative justice dialogue.* LinkedIn. https://www.linkedin.com/advice/3/what-some-common-challenges-pitfalls-avoid-2e

Krznaric, R. (2014). *Empathy heroes: 5 People who changed the world by taking empathy to the extreme.* Yes Magazine. https://www.yesmagazine.org/health-happiness/2014/11/07/empathy-heroes-st-francis-john-howard-griffin-patricia-moore

LaBianca, J. (2022). *10 Inspiring stories of extreme forgiveness that will lift your spirits.* Reader's Digest. https://www.rd.com/list/inspiring-forgiveness-stories/

Lamothe, C. (2023). *How to rescue a damaged relationship.* Healthline. https://www.healthline.com/health/how-to-save-a-relationship#long-distance

Lebow, H.I. (2022). *Letting go of the past: Why it's so hard to get over painful memories.* Psych Central. https://psychcentral.com/health/letting-go-of-the-past-why-memories-remain-painful-over-time

Leo, L. (2023). *10 Ways to embrace vulnerability and grow personally.* Harmony Hustle. https://harmonyhustle.com/2023/10/08/10-ways-to-embrace-vulnerability-and-grow-personally/

Lindberg, S. (2023). *How to forgive yourself.* Health Line. https://www.healthline.com/health/how-to-forgive-yourself

McKenna, A. (n.d.). *15 Nelson Mandela quotes.* Britannica. https://www.britannica.com/list/nelson-mandela-quotes

Moore, M. (2022). *The good kind of vulnerability.* Psych Central. https://psychcentral.com/relationships/the-good-kind-of-vulnerability

Morin, A. (2016). *5 Ways to stop reliving painful memories.* Psychology Today. https://www.psychologytoday.com/us/blog/what-mentally-strong-people-dont-do/201602/5-ways-to-stop-reliving-painful-memories

Pattemore, C. (2021). *10 Ways to build and preserve better boundaries.* Psych Central. https://psychcentral.com/lib/10-way-to-build-and-preserve-better-boundaries

Perina, K. (2013). *9 Steps to forgiveness.* Psychology Today. https://www.psychologytoday.com/us/blog/heart-and-soul-healing/201301/9-steps-forgiveness

Perry, E. (2023). *What is self-preservation? 5 skills for achieving it.* Better Up. https://www.betterup.com/blog/self-preservation-skills

Raypole, C. (2021). *How to find peace of mind: 6 Steps toward lasting serenity.* Psych Central. https://create.dibbly.com/d/Pt9imRoz8egDJbbMZE5D

Richard-Hamilton, F. (2021). *The healing power of nature.* Psychology Today.

https://www.psychologytoday.com/us/blog/the-roots-health/202111/the-healing-power-nature

Ryan. (2023). *15 Journal prompts for letting go of resentment.* The Mindful Page. https://themindfulpage.com/journal-prompts-for-resentment/

Schultz, J. (2020). *Forgiveness therapy: 6+ techniques to help clients forgive.* Positive Psychology. https://positivepsychology.com/forgiveness-in-therapy/#forgiveness-therapy-3-techniques-to-help-clients

Scott, E. (2023). *How spirituality can benefit your health and well-being.* Very Well Mind. https://www.verywellmind.com/how-spirituality-can-benefit-mental-and-physical-health-3144807

Scott, E. (2022). *What is stress?* Very Well Mind. https://www.verywellmind.com/stress-and-health-3145086

Sharma, S. (2023). *7 Key signs that you're on the path to emotional healing.* Calm Sage. https://www.calmsage.com/signs-youre-healing-emotionally/

Sreenivasan, S., & Weinberger, L.E. (2023). *Forever resentful: Grudges are easy to develop, but hard to let go.* Psychology Today. https://www.psychologytoday.com/us/blog/emotional-nourishment/202309/forever-resentful-grudges-are-easy-to-develop-but-hard-to-let-go

Stanborough, S.J. (2023). *Understanding cognitive decline and how your brain changes as you age.* Healthline. https://www.healthline.com/health/cognitive-decline

Tartakovsky, M. (2012). *3 Myths about vulnerability.* Psych Central. https://psychcentral.com/blog/3-myths-about-vulnerability#1

Telloain, S. (2022). *Holding grudges only hurts you. Try these tips to let it go.* Healthline. https://www.healthline.com/health/holding-grudges#the-effects

Toussaint LL, Shields GS, Slavich GM. Forgiveness, stress, and health: a 5-Week Dynamic Parallel Process Study. *Ann Behav Med. 2016;50(5):727-735.* https://doi:10.1007/s12160-016-9796-6

Vanbuskirk, S. (2023). *The mental health affects of holding a grudge.* (2023). Very Well Mind. https://www.verywellmind.com/the-mental-health-effects-of-holding-a-grudge-5176186

Image References

Cyton Photography. (2018). *Two person in long-sleeve shirt handshake* [Image]. Pexels. .https://www.pexels.com/photo/two-person-in-long-sleeved-shirt-shakehand-955395/

Danilyuk, M. (2021). *Unnamed image* [Image]. Pexels. https://www.pexels.com/photo/sitting-blur-reflection-face-6417918/

Danilyuk, M. (2020). *Woman in active wear in yoga pose* [Image]. Pexels. https://www.pexels.com/photo/woman-in-activewear-in-yoga-position-6443466/

Ehlers, M. (2020). *Text on grey background* [Image]. Pexels. https://www.pexels.com/photo/sign-texture-abstract-vintage-4116540/

Grabowska, K. (2020). *Crop woman writing down notes in diary* [Image]. Pexels. https://www.pexels.com/photo/crop-woman-writing-down-notes-in-diary-4476376/

Green, A. (2020). *Black man apologizing while talking with girlfriend* [Image]. Pexels. https://www.pexels.com/photo/black-man-apologizing-while-talking-with-girlfriend-5699848/

Koppens, Y. (2018). *Close-up photography of two clothes pins* [Image]. Pexels. https://www.pexels.com/photo/close-up-photography-of-two-clothespins-776633/

Miroshnichenko, T. (2020). *People sitting on chairs inside room* [Image]. Pexels. https://www.pexels.com/photo/people-sitting-on-chairs-inside-room-5710976/

Moradiya, K. (2020). *Man holding book* [Image]. Pexels. https://www.pexels.com/photo/man-holding-book-2781195/

Piacquadio, A. (2020). *Man showing distress* [Image]. Pexels. https://www.pexels.com/photo/man-showing-distress-3777572/

Pixabay. (2020). *Close-up photo of sad child leaning on a wooden chair* [Image]. Pexels. https://www.pexels.com/photo/close-up-photo-of-sad-child-leaning-on-a-wooden-chair-256657/

Pixabay. (2017). *Question mark on chalkboard* [Image]. Pexels. https://www.pexels.com/photo/question-mark-on-chalk-board-356079/

Ragavan, V. (2018). *Black elephant near trees* [Image]. Pexels https://www.pexels.com/photo/black-elephant-near-trees-982021/

Sackelli, J. (2018). *Green leaf fruit tree selective focal photo* [Image]. Pexels. https://www.pexels.com/photo/green-leaf-fruit-tree-selective-focal-photo-1047312/

Sayles, B. (2018). *Photo of woman wearing white shirt* [Image]. Pexels. https://www.pexels.com/photo/photo-of-woman-wearing-white-shirt-3406020/

Snapwire. (2016). *Man and woman interlocking index fingers with anchor tattoos* [Image]. Pexels. https://www.pexels.com/photo/anchor-couple-fingers-friends-38870/

Subiyanto, K. (2018). *Happy women hugging* [Image]. Pexels. https://www.pexels.com/photo/happy-women-hugging-4584462/

Tiamalu, D. (2019). *Man wearing black long-sleeved shirt standing on mountain* [Image]. Pexels. https://www.pexels.com/photo/man-wearing-black-long-sleeved-shirt-standing-on-mountain-2433291/

Vega, F. (2023). *Seascape with waves and a rope fence on the coast* [Image]. Pexels. https://www.pexels.com/photo/seascape-with-waves-and-a-rope-fence-on-the-coast-17845825/

Volk, J. (2020). *Brown wooden bridge in forest* [Image]. Pexels. https://www.pexels.com/photo/brown-wooden-bridge-in-the-forest-5769699/

Wellington, J. (2016). *Silhouette photo of woman against during golden hour* [Image]. Pexels.

https://www.pexels.com/photo/silhouette-photo-of-woman-against-during-golden-hour-39853/

Wheeler, J. (2018). Photo of pathway surrounded by fir trees [Image]. Pexels. https://www.pexels.com/photo/photo-of-pathway-surrounded-by-fir-trees-1578750/